100 Great Risottos

100 Great Risottos
Valentina Harris

Photographs by Martin Brigdale

CASSELL
ILLUSTRATED

For MP who held my hand

First published in Great Britain in 2003 by Cassell Illustrated,
a division of Octopus Publishing Group Limited,
2-4 Heron Quays, London E14 4JP

Distributed in the United States of America by
Sterling Publishing Co., Inc.,
387 Park Avenue South, New York, NY 10016-8810

A CIP catalogue record for this book is available from the British
Library.

ISBN 1 84403 130 6

Printed in China

Notes on the recipes

Spoon measurements are level.

1 tablespoon is 15 ml; 1 teaspoon is 5 ml.

Eggs are medium.

Wash and dry fresh produce before using.

A wine glass is about 150 ml ($^2/_3$ cup).

A tumbler or glass is about 250 ml (1 cup).

Adjust seasoning or strongly flavoured ingredients to taste.

Contents

A word about the title of this book! I want to apologise to all Italians for the enormous grammatical error and erroneous use of their language... but on occasion my editor won the battle!

Introduction

When I explain to non-Italians about my passion for risotto they tend to look at me with the sort of sceptical expression usually reserved for people who like to breed unusual species of insect in their sitting room! But you see I really do love risotto. I love its texture and its appearance, the way it makes me feel when I eat it and I love its endless, amazing versatility – something that it does share with its other Italian essential first course counterpart: pasta. I love to talk about it, write about it, cook it, eat it and share my passion for it with as many people as possible. I love risotto. Pure and simple.

As I have already said in previous books, my plan is to get as many people as possible, who are not lucky enough to be automatically brought up with a love of risotto ingrained in their soul, to learn to understand and appreciate Italy's great rice dish. It is a one woman campaign, occasionally backed by one or other of the various entities who either grow or market Italian rice, to put risotto on as many tables as possible, all over the world.

This book then, is part of that quest. It was not initially my idea to write another risotto book, but like all great love affairs, we seem to be inextricably linked to one another, so when the offer came up, how could I refuse? It contains mainly entirely new recipes, with a few older recipe ideas revisited and adapted. I am often asked, "How many risotto recipes are there?" and the answer is possibly that these recipes are in fact infinite. Ultimately, all you need is the right kind of rice, an onion, some Parmigiano Reggiano, some good stock and some butter.

With these few ingredients you can create the most basic and simple of all the recipes, Risotto alla Parmigiana, from which

practically all the more complicated and intricate recipes are created. It is a question of building a foundation, and then almost anything goes.

Many people tell me that they are frightened of making risotto because they worry that they will never get the texture quite right. This is a reasonable concern, but easy to overcome. I have, in the course of my lifetime, eaten more risotto than you can possibly imagine, and in doing so have experienced all kinds of different textures. The key is quite simply not to worry about it too much! Risotto can be wet and soupy, dry and somewhat more solid, or anywhere in between. Depending upon what kind of risotto you are inclined to make, the texture will change accordingly. It would be very boring indeed if the texture was always uniform. Changes in texture are dependent upon the kind of rice you use, who is making it, the shape and depth of the pot used, and the level of heat generated from the stove itself, quite apart from the amount of stock used! The important thing is that the rice grains themselves should never be mushy and hopelessly overcooked, nor should they retain any trace of chalkiness, denoting that they have not been sufficiently cooked. The good news is that, once you have got the texture of the cooked rice right, you will always know what you are looking for in the future.

One thing is absolutely certain, and that is that a risotto will be much better if full concentration is given to it during the whole of the cooking process. If you don't give this great dish the attention it deserves, then it will not reward you to the same extent. Just like all love affairs really...

So, whether you are a veteran of the risotto-making fraternity or a novice, I hope very much that this book will become a friend to you in your kitchen, and that it shall at the very least be inspirational for you in terms of risotto experiences.

In my quest to find more recipes, and more ideas for risotto, I have spent a great deal of time looking for other people who felt as passionate as I do about risotto. I am happy to say that this has been a lot easier than I thought it would be. Obviously, more people are starting to appreciate how delicious risotto can be and are cooking it more often at home as well as ordering it in restaurants. This is very heartening indeed, and I hope with all my heart that the interest and love for risotto continues to grow – there is always room in the world for good things like this.

Making and eating risotto

Making risotto should never feel like a chore. However, just like other sensual activities, you really shouldn't bother if you are not in the mood. Life is already filled with enough disappointments, so there really isn't any point in bringing any more upon ourselves. To make risotto well (and to make it a pleasurable and delightful pursuit which you will wish to return to again and again), you need to be in the mood to lose yourself completely to what is going on in the pot. As you stir and gently add the stock to the swelling grains, allowing the smooth velvety texture to swathe around your spoon, you can feel yourself unwind and relax. I always recommend making risotto to stressed-out friends! So, if you are not in the mood, put it off for another time and have a sandwich instead!

What makes a bad risotto - one you will regret working so hard over - is one where the finished risotto is either under- or overcooked, or where the stock was not full-flavoured enough or was overflavoured in comparison with the other ingredients. But if you have the right basic ingredients and adequate equipment to start with, then time, patience and dedication are the only other vital components.

The rice

When I was a little girl living in Italy, there were about 40 different kinds of risotto rice available. One bought risotto rice according to the kind of risotto you wanted to make, and the quality of the individual batches of rice that were harvested. I remember also that one job that always fell to me, or whoever was available at the time, was to sort through the grains. The object was to remove discoloured or shrivelled grains, and to throw out the small stones or pieces of husk or mud that inevitably would be in the sack with the rice. The rice would be measured out and poured on to a surface or into a bowl, then carefully sorted through by letting the grains run between fingers. It was a delightful job which I seldom minded doing, a pleasure which I then grew out of, and now miss again.

Some of my relatives have rice fields where they grow small quantities of rice for their personal use, and sometimes they give

me the odd sack. Although I have to admit that the taste is very much the same as more commonly available varieties, the appearance and feel of it is definitely different, and brings on a rush of the fondest memories for me.

In Italy, you can still buy approximately 12 different kinds of rice for different recipe purposes, whilst elsewhere I have only ever come across the three standard varieties: Arborio, Carnaroli and Vialone Nano. The differences between these three are not easy to distinguish until you actually cook a risotto.

Arborio

The most common type. It is most likely to overcook and will easily disappoint if you are not extra vigilant and careful. This rice is not ideal for risotto virgins!

Vialone Nano

This is the rice type favoured by the Venetians and has a very small hard little grain. The tendency is to use it to make risotti with a slightly soupier texture, and it is popular for fishy recipes. With a far harder grain, it takes slightly longer to cook and has a very different overall texture.

Carnaroli

This rice is considered to be the king of rice varieties, with a huge fat, generous grain that is hard to spoil... by which I mean overcook! In Italy this rice is reserved for very special risotti like truffle or champagne. But, having said that, this is the most dependable variety if you are not an expert, so you can learn to make any kind of risotto with this!

The stock

Whatever kind of risotto you are going to make, just remember that the stock is the second most important ingredient after the rice itself. It should be good enough to drink on its own out of a cup, otherwise it should be saved for making soup instead! If you can, make your own stock using bones, vegetables etc. or you can buy very good quality ready-made chilled stock instead.

If you really must resort to stock cubes or granules, try and find really high quality products and, if possible, those which contain less or no salt and definitely no MSG, so that you have more control over the seasoning.

In all recipes I have suggested using up to 2 litres of stock; you may not use all of this, but I thought you could then make up your own mind as to what sort of texture you want your risotto to have.

Make sure that the stock is hot throughout the cooking process as adding cold stock to the risotto will arrest the cooking process and it will mean that the whole thing takes much longer.

The equipment

Apart from your mood, the other vital items are the right shape and size of pan, a ladle, and a wooden spoon that sits comfortably in the palm of your hand. The saucepan in which you will create your masterpiece needs to be deep enough to prevent too much evaporation, as you want the grains to absorb liquid and flavour, rather than it disappearing into the ether. If the pan is either too shallow or too wide, the liquid will simply evaporate, taking the flavour with it. Twenty minutes of stirring time does not sound very long, but if you haven't got the right equipment it can feel much longer, so make sure the pan and the wooden spoon are compatible with each other and feel comfortable to use. If the saucepan has a heavy bottom, you will find you have better control over the cooking pace.

Finally, the resting time at the end of the cooking is very important, and for this you will need a tight-fitting lid under which the cooked risotto can become even more creamy and delicious than before.

The Italian ingredients

Meat and fish products

Pancetta Salted belly of pork. Similar to bacon.

Prosciutto crudo Cured raw ham such as Parma.

Parma ham The most superior prosciutto crudo from northern Italy.

Luganega A long sausage, often sold in a ring shape, from northern Italy.

Bresaola An air-dried salt beef from Lombardy, usually sold thinly sliced.

Bottarga The cured roe of large fish, such as mullet, tuna or swordfish, air-dried and salted so that it can be shaved or grated.

Cheeses

Pecorino A hard and aged ewe's milk cheese that when sufficiently mature can be grated like Parmigiano Reggiano (Parmesan).

Fontina A cow's milk cheese that is high in fat. The only cheese from the Aosta Valley, it has a melting quality when heated and a very nutty flavour.

Gorgonzola A blue-veined semi-soft cheese that has a creamy texture.

Dolcelatte A young Gorgonzola only made for export, and only by Galbani.

Groviera The Italian version of Gruyère, with the same sweet flavour and melting quality.

Scamorza A mozzarella which has been allowed to drain and become dried out. It can be smoked. Firmer in texture than fresh mozzarella, it has a different flavour and takes longer to melt.

Grana Padano A hard, grating cheese from the Po Valley, similar to Parmigiano Reggiano.

Taleggio A soft, white cow's milk cheese with a distinctive aroma and a fruity flavour, rather ripe, with a slightly powdery rind.

Specialties and alcohol

Mostarda di frutta Candied or glacé fruits in a mustard syrup.

Passata Sieved canned tomatoes, smooth in texture and creamy in consistency.

Limoncello A very sweet and almost sugary, opaque lemon liqueur.

Acquavite A strong spirit made from fruits such as plum, apple, pear etc.

Barolo The most famous Piemontese red wine.

These guidelines are for the majority of risotti in the book, although a few recipes use a different cooking method.

The first thing to do is to choose the correct size of pan. Make sure it is large enough for all the rice once it is cooked, plus the other ingredients included in the recipe.

Prepare all your ingredients before you start to cook. Check your stock for flavour, colour and so on, to make sure that it is the right kind of stock for the risotto you plan to make. Choose the correct rice for the recipe. Heat the stock and keep it just at simmering point.

A step-by-step guide to making risotto

1 Fry the onion, and garlic or other vegetables if using, without allowing them to brown.

2 Add the rice and toast it carefully until shiny, opaque and very hot, but again, without letting it brown. Stir continuously and be patient. Begin to add the wine or first ladleful of hot stock only when the rice is at its hottest.

3 Stir it into the rice and keep stirring until it has all been absorbed. Continue to add the hot stock a ladleful at a time. Always wait for the liquid to be absorbed before adding more. Don't hurry this process; let the rice soak up the liquid and the corresponding flavour at its own pace. Regulate your heat accordingly, keeping the pan over a medium heat. Stir constantly. Gradually you will see that the spoon will leave a clear wake behind it as it is drawn through the risotto. This is a sign of the rice requiring you to add more liquid.

4 The wake will become more obvious the closer the risotto gets to being cooked. It will probably stick to the centre of the pan slightly, which is fine.The risotto is cooked when the texture is velvety but each grain is still firm to the bite in the centre. At this point, take the risotto off the heat, stir in extra butter and/or cheese and cover the pot. Leaving the risotto to rest in this way is called *mantecare* and it makes the texture even more creamy and smooth. After this resting period, turn out on to a warmed platter or warmed individual dishes and serve at once.

The etiquette of eating risotto

Risotto is always traditionally served in a soup plate and is eaten with a fork. You are allowed to press the risotto down with the back of your fork tines in order to help it cool down, but only if you move in a clockwise direction around the plate. Move the plate less that a quarter turn in order to help you achieve this with elegance, and only when necessary.

When it comes to eating it, use your fork in a clockwise direction again, working around the outside of the risotto and gradually into the middle where you will have a little bit left. No Parmigiano is permitted on risotto containing fish, except for very few exceptions. Take small mouthfuls, otherwise you will drop it in your lap and it would be such a shame to waste it! In Martin's lovely pictures, we have used various vessels and bowls, but a soup plate would be more traditional.

What to do with leftovers

As a mother of two huge teenage sons with enormously healthy appetites, I have seldom got any risotto left. On the rare occasions when this does occur, obsessed as I am with not wasting anything, I make these little rice balls:

Arancini di riso

Roll the leftover risotto into balls with your hands, binding the grains together with a little egg if necessary, depending upon how wet and sticky the risotto is to begin with. If you want to, insert a little mozzarella or other cheese into the centre of the ball. Roll in beaten egg and dried breadcrumbs and either shallow fry in sunflower oil or bake off in the oven on oiled baking sheets. Dependent upon their size, you can either serve them as canapés or as a first course or as a light main course with salad.

Comforting Recipes

Cheese, Herbs and Spices

Vegetables and Mushrooms

Fish and Meat

A real classic, and my son Jamie's favourite! You can add more saffron if you want a brighter colour and a more intense taste. Although you can make the risotto with either beef or chicken stock, I prefer to make it with chicken. Jamie is due to start his chef training later this year, I suspect he will be making this a lot!

Some flavour combinations are simply made to be lusted after! They are so perfect that it seems they literally were made for each other. Sage and butter are one of these amazing combinations, usually reserved to dress pasta, but as I happen to love it very much, I have adapted it very successfully to create yet another fabulous risotto.

Risotto with Saffron
Risotto allo Zafferano

1 onion, finely chopped

100 g/4 oz unsalted butter

500 g/1 lb 2 oz risotto rice

1 glass dry white wine

up to 2 litres/8 cups chicken or beef stock, kept simmering

1–3 sachets of saffron powder

75 g/3 oz freshly grated Parmigiano Reggiano

sea salt and freshly milled black pepper

Serves 6

Melt half the butter in a large pan and fry the onion very gently until soft and translucent.

Add the rice and stir until the grains are opaque and very hot, without being browned. Pour in the wine and stir until the liquid has been absorbed and the alcohol has evaporated. Add a ladleful of stock, stir and wait for it to be absorbed, then add more stock and repeat. Continue in this way, always waiting for the rice to absorb the liquid before adding more.

About half way through (when about half the stock has been used), stir the saffron into the rice. When the risotto is velvety and the rice tender but still firm to the bite, remove the pan from the heat and stir in the rest of the butter and the Parmigiano Reggiano.

Adjust the seasoning and cover. Leave to rest for about 3 minutes, then transfer onto a warmed serving platter and serve immediately.

Risotto with Butter and Sage
Risotto Burro e Salvia

50 g/2 oz unsalted butter

1 onion, chopped finely

a handful of fresh sage leaves

350 g/13 oz Arborio rice

1 glass dry white wine

up to 2 litres/8 cups chicken stock, kept hot

60 g/2$\frac{1}{2}$ oz tablespoons freshly grated Parmigiano Reggiano

3 tablespoons extra virgin olive oil

16 perfect, whole fresh sage leaves

sea salt and freshly milled black pepper

Serves 4

Wash and dry the sage leaves; rub them to release the essential oils, then chop them finely. Melt half the butter in a large pan and fry the onion gently until it is soft but not coloured. Add the sage and cook with the onions for a further 2 minutes. Add the rice and toast the grains in the butter and onion until crackling hot.

Add the wine and stir for 1 minute until the alcohol has evaporated, then add 3 ladlefuls of chicken stock and stir until the rice has absorbed most of the liquid. Lower the heat, adding 1$\frac{1}{2}$ ladlefuls of stock at a time and stirring as it is absorbed. After 20 minutes, the rice should be tender but firm to the bite.

Meanwhile, heat the olive oil in a shallow pan and fry the sage leaves until they are just crisp; then drain thoroughly on kitchen paper. Take the cooked risotto off the heat, stir in the remaining butter and almost all the Parmigiano, keeping some back to serve. Taste and season.

Cover and leave to rest for 4 minutes. Transfer on to a warmed serving dish or individual, warmed plates and scatter over the fried sage leaves. Dust with the remaining Parmigiano and serve at once.

Fontina is a very special cheese from Val d'Aosta in northern Italy. It melts to a marvellously gooey texture and has a deliciously nutty flavour and a lovely golden colour.

Risotto with Fontina and Leeks

Risotto di Fontina e Porri

40 g/1½ oz unsalted butter

2 small leeks, trimmed and finely chopped

350 g/13 oz Arborio rice

up to 2 litres/8 cups vegetable or chicken stock, kept simmering

200 g/7 oz Fontina, diced

25 g/2 oz freshly grated Parmigiano Reggiano

sea salt and freshly milled black pepper

Serves 4

In a large pan, fry the leeks very gently in half the butter until they are soft and cooked thoroughly but not browned. Add the rice and cook thoroughly for about 5 minutes, stirring frequently and making sure the grains are well coated and very hot.

Add 3 ladlefuls of stock and stir gently until the rice has absorbed all the liquid. Add more stock, 1½ ladlefuls at a time, each time the spoon leaves a clear wake through the rice.

When the rice is tender but firm to the bite, remove the pan from the heat and stir in the Fontina, the remaining butter and the Parmigiano Reggiano. Season to taste, cover and leave to rest for 4 minutes. Stir and then serve immediately on warmed plates or in a serving dish. Offer more Parmigiano Reggiano separately at the table.

In Valle D'Aosta, many versions of this recipe include a large number of egg yolks and cream, as well as plenty of the wonderfully rich Fontina cheese. This version of the classic recipe is rich without being overwhelming!

Risotto with Fontina

Risotto alla Fontina

100 g/4 oz unsalted butter

1 onion, chopped

1/2 garlic clove, chopped

350 g/13 oz Vialone Nano rice

1 glass fruity white wine (e.g. Reisling)

up to 2 litres/8 cups rich chicken stock, kept simmering

125 g/4 oz diced Fontina

sea salt and freshly milled black pepper

Serves 4

Melt half the butter in a large pan and gently fry the onion and garlic until the onion is so soft that it has almost dissolved.

Raise the heat slightly and add the rice to the pan. Turn the rice in the butter and onion until it is glossy, taking care not to let any of the ingredients brown.

When the rice is hot and beginning to crackle, pour in the wine and stir until the alcohol has evaporated and the rice has absorbed the liquid. Then begin to add the hot stock one ladleful at a time, stirring constantly, only adding more liquid after the previous portion has been absorbed by the rice.

When the rice is about half way through its cooking time (after about 10 minutes), stir in the cheese and mix thoroughly to distribute it evenly through the risotto as it cooks.

Continue to add the stock, making sure that the rice always absorbs the stock before you add more liquid. When the rice is tender but still firm to the bite, adjust the seasoning and make sure that all the cheese has melted through the risotto; then take the pan off the heat.

Stir in the remaining butter, cover and leave the risotto to rest for about 2 minutes. Stir again, then tip onto a warmed platter and serve at once.

It is important that you use a mild, sweet salame like Milano, although you might prefer the stronger spicier taste of a Napoli. If you have not yet discovered Taleggio, it is a soft, gooey cheese from the north of Italy and not unlike Camembert or Brie. I would advise you to remove the rind before dicing it up to put into the risotto.

Risotto with Taleggio and Salame

Risotto con Taleggio e Salame

40 g/1½ oz unsalted butter

1 onion, finely chopped

150 g/5 oz Salame Milano, sliced and cubed

350 g/13 oz Carnaroli rice

1 glass dry white wine

2 litres/8 cups chicken stock, kept simmering

200 g/7 oz Taleggio, cubed

sea salt and freshly milled black pepper

Serves 4

Melt half the butter in a large pan and fry the onion gently in with the salame until the onion is soft and translucent but not browned.

Add the rice, then stir with the other ingredients until it is crackling hot. Add the white wine and allow it to evaporate for 1 minute, stirring. Add 3 ladlefuls of stock and stir again until the stock has been absorbed. Lower the heat and then add another 1½ ladlefuls of stock and stir again until the rice has had the time to absorb the liquid.

Continue in this way until the rice is tender but still firm to the bite. Remove the pan from the heat and add the Taleggio and the remaining butter. Stir and taste, adding seasoning as required, bearing in mind that Salame is quite peppery and salty.

Stir in one final ladle of hot stock and cover. Leave to rest for about 4 minutes, then transfer onto a warmed serving dish or individual plates and eat immediately!

The stinging saltiness of the Gorgonzola is perfect with the walnuts, especially if they are milky and fresh. If the Gorgonzola proves to be too strong, you can always use a milder version such as Dolcelatte.

If you hate blue cheese, then Taleggio, Camembert or Brie can also be used as substitutes, with rind removed.

Risotto with Gorgonzola and Walnuts
Risotto con Gorgonzola e Noci

40 g/1½ oz unsalted butter

1 small onion, peeled and very finely chopped

350 g/13 oz Arborio rice

1 glass dry white wine

up to 2 litres/8 cups chicken or vegetable stock, kept simmering

about 15 walnuts, shelled and coarsely chopped

150 g/5 oz Gorgonzola, diced

sea salt and freshly milled black pepper

Serves 4

Melt half the butter in a large pan. Add the onion and fry gently until the onion is soft but not coloured.

Add the rice and stir thoroughly for about 5 minutes or until the rice is crackling hot. Add the glass of wine and stir for 1–2 minutes until the liquid is absorbed and the alcohol has evaporated. Add 3 ladlefuls of stock and stir until the rice has absorbed the liquid, then add another ladleful of stock and stir. Continue until all the stock has been absorbed or the rice is tender but firm to the bite.

Remove the pan from the heat and stir in the walnuts and Gorgonzola. Mix thoroughly until all the Gorgonzola has melted, then taste and adjust the seasoning, only adding more salt if required. Cover the pan and leave the risotto to rest for 4 minutes, then serve at once on warmed plates or on a serving dish.

The strong taste of ripe Gorgonzola is unmistakable and absolutely delicious. If you find it a little too strong, try using half the quantity. Alternatively, use Dolcelatte, which is simply a young Gorgonzola, although it is only made for export. Follow this risotto with a mouth cleansing salad.

Risotto with Gorgonzola

Risotto al Gorgonzola

100 g/4 oz unsalted butter

1 onion, chopped

$\frac{1}{2}$ teaspoon dried sage

350 g/13 oz risotto rice

up to 2 litres/8 cups chicken or vegetable stock, kept simmering

100 g/4 oz ripe Gorgonzola

2 tablespoons single (light) cream

4 fresh sage leaves, very finely chopped

sea salt and freshly milled black pepper

freshly grated Parmigiano Reggiano, to serve

Serves 4

Melt half the butter in a large pan over a low heat and fry the onion and dried sage until the onion is soft and melting but not browned.

Raise the heat slightly and add the rice. Then stir to thoroughly coat it with the onion, sage and butter, making sure that none of the ingredients brown. Fry until the rice is very hot and beginning to crackle.

Start adding the hot stock a ladleful at a time. Stir constantly and only add more stock when all the liquid has been absorbed. About half way through the cooking time (when about half the stock has been used), stir in the Gorgonzola. Stir thoroughly so that the cheese is evenly distributed into the rice as it quickly melts.

Continue to add the stock, making sure that the rice always absorbs the stock before you add more liquid. When the risotto is creamy and velvety and the rice tender but firm to the bite, remove the pan from the heat and stir in the remaining butter, the cream and the fresh sage. Adjust the seasoning, adding pepper but bearing in mind that the Gorgonzola is very salty and that more may not be needed. Serve immediately on a warmed platter or individual plates and offering freshly grated Parmigiano Reggiano separately.

When I visited Johannesburg last year, I had not been back to South Africa for 7 years, during which time a complete culinary revolution seemed to have taken place in the kitchens of this lovely country. It was especially heart-warming to see risotto on virtually every menu, even if some were strange and unusual variations of the classic dish! This one was not one of those.

Risotto with Feta and Butternut Squash

Risotto con Feta e Zucca

½ small butternut squash

40 g/1½ oz butter

1 onion, finely chopped

2 fresh sage leaves, chopped

350 g/13 oz Arborio rice

1 small glass dry white wine

up to 2 litres/8 cups rich chicken or vegetable stock, kept simmering

200 g/7 oz Feta cheese (pickled cheese), crumbled

a few sage leaves, chopped finely, to garnish

sea salt and freshly milled black pepper

freshly grated Parmigiano Reggiano, to serve

Serves 4

First, bake the whole butternut squash in the oven until it has softened slightly. When it is cool enough to handle, cut it in half. Peel the skin from one half of the squash and scrape away the seeds, then cut the flesh into cubes. Save the other half for soup.

Melt half the butter in a large pan and add the onion, the softened butternut squash and the chopped sage. Fry gently until the onion is soft but not browned. Stir in the rice and allow the grains to cook until the rice starts to crackle and spit.

Add the wine and stir for one minute, allowing the alcohol to evaporate and the liquid to be absorbed. Then add the first 3 ladlefuls of hot stock and stir gently until the grains have absorbed most of the liquid. Continue to add the stock one or two ladlefuls at a time, stirring continuously until all the stock has been absorbed and the rice is tender.

As soon as the rice is cooked, remove it from the heat and stir in the remaining butter until it has melted. Then add the crumbled Feta and stir that through as well. Adjust the seasoning to taste.

Cover and leave to rest for 4 minutes, then serve on warmed plates sprinkled with chopped sage and with the Parmigiano Reggiano offered separately.

This is a springtime recipe, best made with your own tiny carrots from the garden. Certainly it is best to use little carrots bursting with flavour and fresh, tiny peas, freshly podded.

Risotto with Baby Carrots and Peas

Risotto con le Carotine e i Pisellini

40 g/1½ oz unsalted butter

1 onion, chopped, finely

5 baby carrots, washed, scraped and chopped

350 g/13 oz Arborio rice

up to 2 litres/8 cups vegetable stock, kept simmering

5 tablespoons raw fresh peas

50 g/2 oz freshly grated Parmigiano Reggiano

sea salt and freshly milled black pepper

Serves 4

Melt half the butter in a large pan and fry the onion gently for 2–3 minutes, then add the carrots and cook until the onion is soft but not browned.

Add the rice and stir for about 5 minutes until the rice is crackling hot. Then add 3 ladlefuls of stock and stir until the rice has absorbed almost all the liquid. Continue to add the stock 1–1½ ladlefuls at a time only adding more liquid when the last has been absorbed by the rice.

After about 10 minutes, when the rice is half cooked, add the peas and continue to cook as before. When the rice is tender but still firm to the bite, remove the pan from the heat. Stir in a final ladleful of stock, 3 tablespoons of the Parmigiano Reggiano, and season to taste. Cover and leave to rest for about 4 minutes, then stir again. Transfer onto a warmed platter or individual plates, sprinkle with the remaining cheese and serve at once.

The striking thing about this risotto is, of course, the amazing heliotrope colour. Make sure that you use beetroot that has been cooked in water and not in vinegar! If you cook your own, take care not to boil it for too long or the beetroot will begin to go pale and its colour will be uneven and mottled.

Risotto with Beetroot

Risotto di Rape Rosse

75 g/3 oz unsalted butter	Melt half the butter in a large pan and fry the onion gently until soft but not coloured. Add the beetroot and stir.
1 large onion, finely chopped	
500 g/1 lb 2 oz boiled, peeled beetroot (beet), diced	When the beetroot is beginning to go soft and limp, add the rice and stir thoroughly, until the rice begins to crackle. Pour over the Vermouth and allow it evaporate for one minute, stirring the rice all the time. Begin to add the stock in the usual way, stirring and waiting for the rice to absorb the liquid before adding more.
500 g/1 lb 2 oz Arborio rice	
½ glass dry Vermouth	Half way through the cooking time, season to taste then continue to cook the risotto until it is creamy and the rice is tender but firm to the bite. Take the pan off the heat, stir in the remaining butter, the herbs and the Parmigiano Reggiano. Cover and leave the risotto to rest for 2–3 minutes, then transfer onto a warmed platter and serve immediately.
up to 2 litres/8 cups chicken stock or light duck stock, kept simmering	
3 tablespoons finely chopped fresh chives	
3 tablespoons finely chopped fresh flat leaf parsley	
75 g/3 oz freshly grated Parmigiano Reggiano	
sea salt and freshly milled black pepper	
Serves 4 to 6	

The secret to this recipe is to use really tender, sweet-tasting vegetables. Make sure that there are some beetroot or turnip tops in with the vegetables to add some green to the finished dish.

Risotto with Baby Turnips and Beetroot

Risotto con le Rape Bianche e Rosse

50 g/2 oz unsalted butter

1 onion, finely chopped

5 baby turnips, cubed

5 green turnip tops, washed and shredded (optional)

350 g/13 oz Arborio rice

1 small beetroot (beet), baked in its skin, like a jacket potato

green tops from beetroot (beet), if available, washed and shredded

up to 2 litres/8 cups chicken or vegetable stock, kept simmering

50 g/2 oz freshly grated Parmigiano Reggiano

sea salt and freshly milled black pepper

Serves 4

Melt half the butter in a large pan and gently fry the onion and turnip until softened but not browned. Add the rice and stir, toasting the grains in the butter for about 4 minutes, until crackling hot. Scrape out all the flesh from the baked beetroot and mix with the rice.

Add 3 ladlefuls of stock. Stir until the rice has absorbed most of the liquid. Continue to add the stock $1-1\frac{1}{2}$ ladlefuls at a time, stirring to allow the rice to absorb the liquid before adding more. When almost at the end of the cooking time, add the shredded turnip tops, if using, and continue to cook the risotto as before.

When the rice is tender but still firm to the bite, remove the pan from the heat and stir in the remaining butter. Adjust the seasoning and add the grated Parmigiano Reggiano; then cover and leave to rest for 4 minutes. Stir in a final half-ladleful of stock and transfer on to a warmed serving dish or individual plates. Serve at once, with more freshly grated Parmigiano Reggiano offered separately.

This is a very English risotto, which just proves that as long as you get the technique right, and balance the flavours carefully, you can make a risotto with almost any good ingredients. You can substitute potato for the parsnip and Roquefort or other blue cheese for the Stilton.

If you really cannot find pancetta, you can substitute best-quality smoked streaky (fatty) bacon, although nothing quite matches the taste of the real thing.

Risotto with Parsnip and Stilton

Risotto con le Rape Dolci e Formaggio Stilton

Risotto with Potato

Risotto di Patate

50 g/2 oz unsalted butter	Melt half the butter in a large pan and gently fry the leek with the parsnips until the leek is soft but not browned.
1 leek, trimmed and finely chopped	
2 tender young parsnips, peeled and grated	Add the rice and cook until it is crackling hot then add the glass of sherry and stir until the alcohol has evaporated. Then add 3 ladlefuls of stock and stir until the rice has absorbed most of the liquid. As soon as the rice starts to dry out, add another $1\frac{1}{2}$ ladlefuls of stock and cook as before. Continue to add the stock until the rice is tender but firm to the bite.
350 g/13 oz Arborio rice	
1 small glass dry sherry	
up to 2 litres/8 cups chicken or vegetable stock, kept hot	
100 g/4 oz mature Stilton, crumbled	
sea salt and freshly milled black pepper	Stir in the remaining butter and the Stilton and mix with the rice until both have melted. Taste and adjust the seasoning. Stir in one more ladleful of stock then cover and leave to rest for about 4 minutes. Transfer the risotto onto individual plates or a warmed platter and serve.
Serves 4	

125 g/4 oz pancetta, chopped	In a large pan, gently fry the pancetta, onion, parsley and rosemary until the onion is transparent and soft. Add the potatoes and stir, adding a little stock to cook the potatoes until they lose their raw appearance.
1 large onion, chopped	
a handful of chopped fresh flat leaf parsley	
1 tablespoon finely chopped fresh rosemary leaves	Add the rice and stir until the grains are shiny and opaque. Add the first ladleful of stock and stir until the rice has absorbed the liquid, then add more stock. Continue in this way until the rice is creamy and smooth but still firm to the bite.
300 g/11 oz potatoes, peeled and cubed	
up to 2 litres/8 cups beef or game stock, kept simmering	
400 g/14 oz Arborio rice	
50 g/2 oz unsalted butter	Remove the pan from the heat and season to taste. Stir in the butter and cheeses and cover. Rest for 3 minutes and mix again, making sure the Groviera is melted and stringy, then turn on to a warmed platter or individual plates and serve at once.
50 g/2 oz Groviera or Gruyère, finely cubed	
75 g/3 oz freshly grated Parmigiano Reggiano	
sea salt and freshly milled black pepper	
Serves 4 to 6	

Luganega is a thin, continuous coil Italian sausage. It is quite coarse and has a fairly strong taste. If you can't get hold of it, use any other kind of raw Italian sausage, half the quantity of finely chopped pancetta or smoked streaky bacon.

Risotto with Spinach and Walnut

Risotto di Spinaci con le Noci

600 g/1 lb 5 oz fresh spinach

75 g/3 oz unsalted butter

1 onion, finely chopped

150g/5 oz Luganega sausage, skinned and crumbled or pancetta, chopped

400 g/14 oz Arborio rice

1 glass dry white wine

up to 2 litres/8 cups beef or chicken stock, kept simmering

40 g/2 oz finely chopped walnuts

75g/3 oz freshly grated Parmigiano Reggiano

sea salt and freshly milled black pepper

Serves 4

Wash the spinach thoroughly, then steam briefly until just wilted. Drain thoroughly, squeeze dry and then chop finely.

Melt half the butter in a large pan and fry the onion and sausage or bacon until the onion is soft and transparent. Add the rice and stir for a few minutes until the rice is mixed with the other ingredients and crackling hot.

Add the wine and stir until the alcohol has evaporated. Reduce the heat and add 3 ladlefuls of stock. Stir until the rice has absorbed the liquid then add more stock, about $1\frac{1}{2}$ ladlefuls at a time, waiting for the rice to absorb the liquid and only adding more when the previous quantity has been absorbed.

Continue to stir and add stock gradually until the rice is half cooked (after about 10 minutes) and then add the spinach. Stir and adjust the seasoning and continue to add the stock and cook the rice as before. When the rice is tender but still firm to the bite, remove from the heat, stir in the walnuts, the remaining butter and the Parmigiano Reggiano. Cover and leave to rest for 2–3 minutes, then serve immediately on a warmed platter.

This is a lovely, old-fashioned risotto that is lifted by the distinctive taste of caraway. The recipe comes from the Friuli region in Italy where caraway is very popular.

Risotto with Savoy Cabbage

Risotto di Verze

75 g/3 oz unsalted butter or pork dripping

1 onion, finely chopped

700 g/1 lb 9 oz risotto rice

2 glasses dry white wine, such as Soave

up to 2 litres/8 cups good-quality chicken or vegetable stock, kept simmering

400 g/14 oz finely shredded Savoy cabbage

1 level teaspoon caraway seeds, (optional)

125 g/4 oz freshly grated Parmigiano Reggiano

sea salt and freshly milled black pepper

Serves 6 to 8

Melt the butter or dripping in a large pan and fry the onion gently until it is softened but not browned.

Add the risotto rice and cook until it is very hot and has started to crackle. Add the wine and stir until the alcohol has evaporated and the liquid has been absorbed. Then add one ladleful of stock, stirring constantly until it has been absorbed.

After 10 minutes, add the cabbage. Stir thoroughly, and continue to add the stock as before until the rice is tender. Add the caraway seeds now, if you like the taste of them.

Remove the pan from the heat and season to taste. Then add half the cheese and stir again. Cover and leave the risotto to rest for about 3 minutes.

Transfer the risotto to a warmed serving dish or individual warmed plates, sprinkle with the remaining Parmigiano Reggiano and serve. Alternatively, serve the risotto in a cup of blanched outer leaves from the cabbage. For a really dramatic effect, serve on blanched red cabbage leaves.

Red cabbage is one of those marvellous vegetables that work incredibly well with spices like cinnamon and clove. In this risotto, spices and red wine are used quite liberally in order to make the most of all the flavours available.

Risotto with Red Cabbage

Risotto al Cavolo Rosso

50 g/2 oz unsalted butter

1 red onion, finely chopped

$\frac{1}{2}$ sweet dessert apple, peeled and cubed

$\frac{1}{4}$ teaspoon ground cinnamon

a pinch of ground cloves

a large pinch of ground nutmeg

200 g/7 oz red cabbage, very finely chopped

350 g/13 oz Arborio rice

1 large glass of dry red wine

up to 2 litres/8 cups chicken stock, kept hot

50 g/2 oz freshly grated Parmigiano Reggiano

sea salt and freshly milled black pepper

Serves 4

Melt half the butter in a large pan and fry the onion with the apple and all the spices for about 5 minutes, or until the onion and the apple are soft and cooked through, but not browned. Add the cabbage and stir, cooking gently for another 5 to 10 minutes or until softened.

Add the rice, stirring continuously for about 5 minutes until the grains are crackling hot, then add the red wine. Stir for a further 2 minutes until the alcohol has evaporated, then add 3 ladlefuls of stock and continue to stir until the rice has absorbed most of the liquid, then lower the heat and continue to add stock, a ladleful at a time, until the rice is tender but still firm to the bite.

Remove the pan from the heat, mix in the remaining butter and half the Parmigiano Reggiano. Stir again and season to taste then cover and leave to rest for about 4 minutes. Stir once more and transfer to a warmed serving dish and sprinkle with the remaining Parmigiano Reggiano.

This risotto is lovely to look at, but as well as being pretty it is very simple to make and comforting to eat as it is mild and doesn't present too much of a challenge to most people's tastebuds.

Risotto with Peas and Saffron

Risotto con i Pisellini e Zafferano

75 g/3 oz unsalted butter

1 small onion, peeled and very finely chopped

4 handfuls frozen peas

350 g/13 oz Arborio rice

up to 2 litres/8 cups chicken or vegetable stock, kept simmering

a pinch of saffron threads or 2 sachets of saffron powder

50 g/2 oz freshly grated Parmigiano Reggiano

sea salt and freshly milled black pepper

Serves 4

If using saffron threads, start by soaking them in warm water for 30 minutes, then strain, reserving the liquid. Discard threads.

Melt half the butter in a large pan and fry the onion gently until softened but not coloured.

Add all the rice and quickly fry the grains in the butter and onion for up to 5 minutes or until the rice is crackling hot, but not browned. Add 3 ladlefuls of hot stock and stir thoroughly. Add 3 handfuls of peas and cook for 2–3 minutes stirring continuously until all the stock has been absorbed. Add more stock, $1\frac{1}{2}$ ladlefuls at a time, stirring until each quantity of stock has been absorbed.

When the rice is tender but firm to the bite, take the pan off the heat. Stir in the remaining butter and peas, the saffron powder or strained infusion from the saffron threads, seasoning to taste and half the Parmigiano Reggiano. Stir thoroughly, then cover and leave to stand for 4 minutes. Stir again and transfer onto a warmed serving dish or individual plates, sprinkle with the remaining cheese and serve at once.

This recipe is cooked in the old way, without frying the onion in fat at the beginning of the recipe. The end result is really a very thick soup rather than a risotto.

Venetian Rice and Peas

Risi e Bisi

1 kg/2 lb 4 oz fresh peas in the pod (pod peas) or 500 g/ 1 lb 2 oz frozen petit pois, defrosted

$^1/_2$ mild, sweet onion, very finely chopped

50 g/2 oz pancetta, chopped

$1^1/_2$ tablespoons extra virgin olive oil

50 g/2 oz unsalted butter

25 g/1 oz chopped fresh parsley

up to 2 litres/8 cups good-quality beef, veal or chicken stock, kept simmering

300 g/11 oz rice, preferably Vialone Nano Gigante if available

50 g/2 oz freshly grated Parmigiano Reggiano

sea salt and freshly milled black pepper

Serves 4

If you are using fresh peas, shell all the peas carefully and give them a quick rinse in cold water.

In a large pan, fry the onion and pancetta in the olive oil and butter, for about 10 minutes. Add the parsley and stir. Fry slowly for a further 4 minutes, then add the peas and stir thoroughly. Add just enough stock to barely cover, then simmer very slowly until the peas begin to get tender.

Add the rice, stir and add more stock. Season and stir again, waiting for the grains to absorb the stock before adding more liquid. When the rice is soft and tender but firm to the bite, remove the pan from the heat, stir in the cheese and rest for 3 minutes before turning into warmed bowls or a warmed tureen to serve. Offer extra grated Parmigiano Reggiano at the table.

A very substantial winter risotto, enhanced by the fresh sage leaves that release their pungent flavours into the butter. You can boil your own beans or buy them ready cooked and canned.

Risotto with Beans and Pancetta

Risotto con i Fagioli e la Pancetta

75 g/3 oz unsalted butter

1 large onion, finely chopped

200 g/7 oz smoked pancetta, cubed

5 large fresh sage leaves, finely chopped

350 g/13 oz Arborio rice

1 large glass dry red wine

up to 2 litres/8 cups chicken stock, kept simmering

350 g/13 oz cooked borlotti or haricot (navy) beans, drained

60 g/ 2½ oz freshly grated Parmigiano Reggiano or Grana Padano

sea salt and freshly milled black pepper

Serves 4

Melt half the butter in a large pan. Add the onion, half the pancetta and the sage leaves, then fry gently until the onion is soft but not browned. This is difficult to achieve as the pancetta needs to melt without browning or going crisp, but try not to let the onion brown too much.

Add the rice and toast the grains, stirring for about 5 minutes or until they are crackling hot. Add the glass of red wine and stir for 1 minute or until the alcohol has evaporated. Add 3 ladlefuls of hot stock and stir until the rice has absorbed most of the liquid.

As soon as the rice begins to dry out, lower the heat and add the beans. Then continue cooking the rice as before, adding 1–1½ ladles of stock at a time and stirring until it has been absorbed by the rice. In a separate pan, dry fry the remaining pancetta cubes until brown and crunchy. Reserve until required.

When the rice is cooked through but still firm to the bite, take the risotto off the heat. Stir in the remaining butter, the fried pancetta cubes and half the cheese. Cover and leave to rest for about 4 minutes. Stir again and transfer to a warmed serving dish or warmed plates. Serve sprinkled with the remaining cheese and garnished with sprigs of fresh sage.

This risotto differs from the others — where the onion has to be chopped finely so that it virtually disappears. In this dish, the red onion is the main flavouring, so you can afford for it to be a much more visible part of the whole dish.

You can vary the amount of garlic that you use for this tasty recipe, using more or less than 5 cloves, depending on your own preferences and circumstances.

Risotto with Red Onion

Risotto di Cipolle Rosse

50 g/2 oz unsalted butter	Melt half the butter in a large pan and fry the onions gently until they are soft but not browned.
3 red onions, thinly sliced	
350 g/13 oz Arborio rice	Add all the rice and toast the grains with the onions and the butter, stirring frequently for about 5 minutes until the rice is crackling hot. Next, add the wine and stir for about 2 minutes until the alcohol has evaporated. Then add 3 ladlefuls of hot stock and stir until the rice has absorbed the liquid. Turn down the heat and begin to add more stock, 1½ ladlefuls at a time, stirring until absorbed by the rice each time.
1 glass dry white wine	
up to 2 litres/8 cups fresh vegetable or chicken stock, kept simmering	
50 g/2 oz freshly grated Parmigiano Reggiano	
2 tablespoons chopped fresh flatleaf parsley	
sea salt and freshly milled black pepper	Continue in this way until the rice is tender but firm to the bite. Take the pan off the heat, stir in the remaining butter, the Parmigiano Reggiano, the parsley and the seasoning. Cover and leave to rest for about 4 minutes, then transfer to a warmed serving dish or plates and serve at once.
Serves 4	

Risotto with Garlic

Risotto all'aglio

5 tablespoons extra virgin olive oil (preferably Ligurian)	In a large pan, gently fry the garlic and parsley in the oil for about 5 minutes or until the garlic is softened. Season to taste with salt and pepper then add the ham and tomatoes, stirring to break them up. When the mixture is hot and bubbling, add the rice and continue to stir until well combined with the other ingredients.
5 garlic cloves, finely chopped	
a large handful of fresh flat leaf parsley, de-stalked and finely chopped	
100 g/4 oz canned tomatoes, drained	
75 g/3 oz coarsely chopped ham	Next, start adding the stock one ladleful at a time, stirring continuously and waiting until all the liquid has been absorbed before adding more. Continue in this way until the rice is tender but firm to the bite.
500 g/1 lb 2 oz Arborio rice	
up to 2 litres/8 cups vegetable stock, kept simmering	
50 g/2 oz freshly grated Parmigiano Reggiano, plus extra to serve	Take the pan off the heat, stir in the Parmigiano Reggiano and leave to rest, covered, for about 4 minutes. Transfer to a warmed platter and serve at once. Offer extra Parmigiano Reggiano separately at the table.
sea salt and freshly milled black pepper	
Serves 4	

A risotto that has everything: a fabulous hue and a great taste. It is made using the much underrated pumpkin, although butternut squash is a good substitute.

Risotto with Pumpkin
Risotto con la Zucca

75 g/3 oz thickly cut and cubed pancetta or top-quality smoked streaky (fatty) bacon

2 tablespoons olive oil

1 medium-sized onion, chopped

500 g/1 lb 2 oz pumpkin, peeled, seeded and chopped

400 g/14 oz risotto rice

up to 2 litres/8 cups vegetable or chicken stock, kept simmering

a handful of finely chopped fresh parsley

25 g/1 oz unsalted butter

40 g/1½ oz freshly grated Parmigiano Reggiano

sea salt and freshly milled black pepper

Serves 4

Fry the pancetta gently in a large pan, in the olive oil until the fat runs, then add the onion and fry until softened. Add the pumpkin and cook until soft and mushy.

Add the rice and heat until crackling hot, then start to add the stock one ladleful at a time, stirring until the rice has absorbed most of the liquid. Add more stock gradually until the rice is tender but firm to the bite.

Season to taste and stir in the parsley, butter and Parmigiano Reggiano. Remove the pan from the heat and cover. Leave to stand for 3 minutes, then transfer to a warmed platter and serve at once.

The inspiration for this recipe comes from a favourite soup in which Camembert or Brie is melted in to a purée of Cannellini beans, stock and milk. With a few changes, it is a combination that works amazingly well in a risotto too.

Risotto with Cannellini Beans and Camembert

Risotto con i Cannellini e il Camembert

40 g/1½ oz unsalted butter

1 onion or leek, finely chopped

2 tablespoons finely chopped fresh flat leaf parsley

350 g/13 oz Arborio rice

1 glass dry white wine

400 g/14 oz can cannellini beans, drained and rinsed

up to 2 litres/8 cups chicken or vegetable stock, kept simmering

200 g/7 oz Camembert or Brie, rind removed and cubed

sea salt and freshly milled black pepper

Serves 4

Melt half the butter in a large pan and fry the onion or leek until soft but not browned. Add the parsley and the rice, and stir until the rice is very hot and crackling.

Add the wine and allow the alcohol to evaporate for 1 minute before adding the beans and 3 ladlefuls of stock. Stir until the liquid has almost been completely absorbed, then lower the heat and begin to add more stock, adding about 1½ ladlefuls at a time. Stir constantly to prevent the rice from sticking and cook until all the stock has been absorbed and the beans are very soft and overcooked and start to disintegrate.

When the rice is tender, take the pan off the heat and stir in the cheese until it melts. Season to taste with the salt and pepper and add one more ladleful of hot stock. Stir again, cover and leave to rest for about 4 minutes. Give the risotto a final stir and then serve on individual warmed plates or on a warmed serving dish.

A fresh and nourishing risotto with an interesting combination of
Mediterranean flavours. The chickpeas add texture and take on the
taste of the garlic really well. It's especially good with a tomato salad
dressed with olive oil and plenty of dried oregano.

Risotto with Chickpeas and Parsley

Risotto con i Ceci e Prezzemolo

4 garlic cloves, crushed

5 tablespoons extra virgin olive oil

350g/13 oz Arborio rice

up to 2 litres/8 cups chicken or vegetable stock, kept simmering

250 g/9 oz cooked or canned chick peas, drained and rinsed

a large handful of chopped fresh flat leaf parsley

25 g/1 oz freshly grated Parmigiano Reggiano or Pecorino, plus extra to serve

sea salt and freshly milled black pepper

Serves 4

In a large pan, fry the garlic gently in 4 tablespoons of the olive oil until just softened but not browned, then add the rice. Stir the rice in the oil and garlic until it is thoroughly coated in the oil and crackling hot.

Then add the first 3 ladlefuls of stock and stirring continuously. Lower the heat and continue to cook, adding stock 1–2 ladlefuls at a time and stirring constantly.

After 10 minutes, add the chick peas and continue to cook as before, adding the stock until the rice is tender but not soft. Remove the pan from the heat and mix in the remaining tablespoon of extra virgin olive oil, the parsley (reserving a little for garnishing) and the Parmigiano Reggiano or Pecorino. Stir and adjust the seasoning to taste, then cover and leave the risotto to rest for about 4 minutes.

Stir again and then serve on a warmed platter, sprinkled with a little more parsley and with the grated Parmigiano or Pecorino offered separately.

If you can find it, sheep's milk ricotta is the best choice for this risotto as it tends to have a slightly more vivid flavour. In any case, the stock needs to really pack a punch, so make sure it is quite intensely flavoured for the best results, but watch the saltiness!

Risotto with Spinach and Ricotta

Risotto di Spinaci e Ricotta

1 onion, very finely chopped

40 g/1½ oz unsalted butter

350 g/13 oz Arborio rice

up to 2 litres/8 cups full-flavoured chicken or vegetable stock, kept simmering

350 g/13 oz raw baby spinach leaves, coarsely chopped

a little freshly grated nutmeg, to taste

40 g/1½ oz fresh ricotta

75 g/3 oz freshly grated Parmigiano Reggiano

sea salt and freshly milled black pepper

Serves 4

Melt half the butter in a large pan and very gently fry the onion until it is softened but not coloured.

Raise the heat a little and add all the rice. Stir the rice until it is so hot that it crackles, but take care to ensure that it does not brown. Add 3 ladlefuls of stock and stir until the rice has absorbed most of the liquid. Lower the heat and continue to cook the rice, adding stock and stirring thoroughly between each addition, waiting each time for the rice to absorb the stock.

When the rice is tender but still firm to the bite, remove the pan from the heat. Stir in the chopped spinach, the nutmeg and the ricotta, and mix together thoroughly. Then add the remaining butter and half the Parmigiano Reggiano and stir again.

Cover and leave the risotto to rest for about 4 minutes, then stir again. Transfer onto a warmed dish or individual plates and serve sprinkled with the remaining Parmigiano Reggiano.

There are many versions of this classic risotto because so many people seem to love it more than any other! Here is my own version, which uses a touch of garlic and rosemary to really bring out the flavour of the mushrooms. If you cannot find wild mushrooms, use ordinary cultivated mushrooms instead. For a really strong mushroom flavour you can, of course, use dried porcini mushrooms, too.

Risotto with Mushrooms

Risotto con i Funghi

200 g/7 oz mixed wild mushrooms

75 g/3 oz unsalted butter

1 onion, chopped

1–2 garlic cloves, chopped

1 small sprig of fresh rosemary, chopped

1 large glass dry white wine

350 g/13 oz Arborio rice

up to 2 litres/8 cups chicken or vegetable stock, kept simmering

sea salt and freshly milled black pepper

freshly grated Grana Padano or Parmesan, to serve

Serves 4

Check the mushrooms carefully, making sure that they are clean and free of any dirt or debris; wipe them clean if necessary and trim off any hard corners before chopping coarsely.

Melt half the butter in a large pan and gently fry the onion, garlic and rosemary until the onion is soft. Add the mushrooms and mix thoroughly with the other ingredients in the pan, cooking until the mushrooms are just soft.

Add the white wine and stir. Wait for the alcohol to evaporate, then add the rice and seasoning. Heat the rice until it begins to crackle. Add the stock a ladleful at a time, stirring continuously and waiting until the liquid has been absorbed before you add the next quantity of stock.

Continue in this way until the rice is tender but firm to the bite. Remove the pan from the heat and stir in the remaining butter. Cover the pan and leave the risotto to stand for about 3 minutes before transferring to a warmed platter to serve. Offer Grana Padano or Parmigiano Reggiano separately. If the mushrooms are very strong the cheese may not be needed.

A very rich combination of flavours and textures and not a risotto for anyone who is anything less than starving hungry! Plenty of dry red wine is essential for this dish, and follow the risotto with a very refreshing salad. Delicious, but it needs hearty appetites!

Risotto with Mushrooms and Chicken Livers

Risotto con i Funghi e i Fegatini di Pollo

40 g/1½ oz unsalted butter

1 large onion, finely chopped

1½ large garlic cloves, finely chopped

200 g/7 oz coarsely chopped mushrooms

2 fresh sage leaves, very finely chopped

350 g/13 oz Arborio or Carnaroli rice

1 glass dry white wine

up to 2 litres/8 cups chicken or vegetable stock, kept simmering

2 tablespoons extra virgin olive oil

200 g/7 oz chicken livers, coarsely chopped

½ glass brandy

25 g/2 oz freshly grated Parmigiano Reggiano

sea salt and freshly milled black pepper

Serves 4

Melt half the butter in a large pan and add the onion, two-thirds of the garlic and the mushrooms. As soon as the onions have begun to sizzle, add the sage leaves. Stir and simmer together gently, adding a little bit of stock, if necessary, to prevent any sticking.

Add the rice and heat until crackling hot. Add the wine and remove the pan from the heat until the alcohol has evaporated. Return the pan to the heat and add 3 ladlefuls of stock. Allow the rice to absorb the liquid, then add about 1½ ladlefuls at time, waiting for the rice to absorb the liquid before adding more.

Meanwhile, warm the olive oil in a small pan with the remaining garlic, until the aroma of the garlic is quite strong, then add in the chicken livers and stir to brown all over. Add the brandy and ignite the alcohol to burn off the fumes, then season with salt and pepper. Lower the heat and cook, uncovered, for 1–2 minutes, but no longer or the chicken livers will become rubbery. Remove the pan from the heat and set aside until required.

As soon as the rice is tender but firm to the bite, remove the pan from the heat. Stir in the remaining butter and the Parmigiano Reggiano cheese and adjust the seasoning to taste. Add a bit more stock to prevent the risotto from drying out, then cover and leave to rest for about 4 minutes.

Briefly warm the chicken livers over a high heat. Stir the risotto then transfer onto a warmed platter. Arrange the chicken livers over the top and serve at once, with extra Parmigiano Reggiano offered separately.

A deliciously mild, buttery, lightly fishy risotto which is complimented brilliantly by the freshly chopped flat leaf parsley showered in right at the very end. An ideal way to use up any leftover fish you might have.

Risotto with Creamy Fish

Risotto Cremoso al Pesce

1 leek, trimmed and finely chopped

50 g/2 oz unsalted butter

350 g/13 oz Vialone Nano rice

1 glass dry white wine

up to 2 litres/8 cups fish stock

200 g/7 oz cooked white fish, skinned, boned and flaked

3 tablespoons freshly chopped fresh flat leaf parsley

sea salt and freshly milled black pepper

Serves 4

Melt half the butter in a large pan and fry the leek very gently until soft.

Add the rice and mix thoroughly with the other ingredients for a few minutes or until crackling hot. Add the wine and stir for 1 minute, then add 3 ladlefuls of fish stock and stir until the rice has absorbed most of the liquid.

Turn down the heat and add the fish and another $1\frac{1}{2}$ ladles of fish stock. Continue to cook the rice, gradually adding stock $1\frac{1}{2}$ ladles at a time and stirring constantly.

When the rice is tender but still firm to the bite, remove the pan from the heat and add the butter. Stir and then adjust the seasoning. Cover and rest for 4 minutes, then mix in a little more stock to keep the risotto moist. Finally, stir in the parsley and serve at once.

This is a real warmer for cold evenings, made even more nourishing and satisfying by the addition of a perfectly cooked poached egg.

Risotto with Smoked Haddock and Poached Eggs

Risotto con Pesce Affumicato e Uova in Camicia

40 g/1½ oz unsalted butter	Melt half the butter in a large pan and fry the leek gently (make sure it doesn't brown).
1 small leek, trimmed and finely chopped	Add the rice stirring constantly, for about 5 minutes until it is crackling hot. Then add 3 ladlefuls of hot stock and stir until the rice has absorbed the liquid. Lower the heat and continue for another 10 minutes. Next, add the cooked, flaked haddock and when it has been thoroughly mixed in to the risotto, add the milk. Continue to add the stock 1–1½ ladlefuls at a time, waiting each time for the liquid to be absorbed before adding more.
350 g/13 oz Arborio rice	
up to 2 litres/8 cups vegetable stock, kept simmering	
200 g/7 oz poached smoked haddock, skinned and flaked, all bones removed	
250ml/1 cup full-fat (whole) milk	
a dash of white wine vinegar	When the risotto is tender but still firm to the bite, remove it from the heat and stir in the remaining butter and half the parsley. Season to taste with salt and pepper. Cover and leave to rest.
4 fresh free-range (farm-fresh) eggs	
50 g/2 oz finely chopped fresh flat leaf parsley	
sea salt and freshly milled black pepper	Meanwhile, fill a shallow pan with hot water and add the vinegar. Bring to simmering point and poach the eggs, by slipping them carefully into the boiling water.
Serves 4	

When the eggs are cooked, stir the risotto one more time, then transfer on to 4 warmed soup plates. Lay a poached egg on each portion of risotto and sprinkle with chopped parsley. Serve at once.

Italian canned tuna is far superior to any other, so try to buy a brand like Palmera, Callipo or Rio Mare if you can. Also, make sure the tuna is canned in olive oil and not brine.

Risotto with Tuna Fish

Risotto con il Tonno

125 g/4 oz unsalted butter	Melt a third of the butter in a large pan and fry the onion gently until soft and translucent. Add the rice and stir to coat it thoroughly in the butter and onion.
1 large onion, finely chopped	
500 g/1 lb 2 oz Arborio rice	
1 glass dry white wine	When the rice is opaque and very hot but not browned, add the wine. Let the alcohol evaporate, stirring all the time then add the stock a ladleful at a time, stirring after each addition and making sure that all the liquid is absorbed before adding any more. Season to taste and continue to cook in the same way.
up to 2 litres/8 cups vegetable stock, kept simmering	
2 tablespoons plain white (all purpose) flour	
500 ml/2½ cups full-fat (whole) milk	
125 g/4 oz canned tuna in olive oil, drained and flaked	Meanwhile, melt the remaining butter in a separate pan until foaming, taking care not to brown. Add the flour and stir to a paste, then add the milk and whisk energetically to prevent any lumps from forming. Season and simmer for about 10 minutes or until quite thick. Taste to check that there is no taste of flour. Add the flaked tuna and the parsley, stir and remove the pan from the heat.
4 tablespoons finely chopped fresh parsley	
sea salt and freshly milled black pepper	
Serves 4	

When the risotto is creamy and the rice tender but still firm to the bite, transfer it onto a warmed platter. Pour the tuna sauce over the risotto and serve at once.

A very filling, substantial, risotto that is perfect for cold winter evenings. Do make sure that you use the best quality, leanest beef available.

Risotto with Beef and Mushrooms

Risotto con Manzo e Funghi

40 g/1½ oz unsalted butter

1 onion, finely chopped

200 g/7 oz trimmed stewing steak, finely diced

1 small carrot, finely chopped

1 small celery stick, finely chopped

200 g/7 oz cleaned mushrooms, sliced

1 tablespoon tomato purée, diluted in a little warm water

1 glass red wine

350 g/13 oz Arborio rice

up to 2 litres/8 cups beef stock, kept simmering

50 g/2 oz freshly grated Parmigiano Reggiano

2 tablespoons chopped fresh flat leaf parsley

sea salt and freshly milled black pepper

Serves 4

Melt half the butter in a large pan. Add the onion, steak, carrot, celery, mushrooms and tomato purée and fry gently until the onion is soft and all the ingredients cooked but not browned. Keep everything moist as you cook it by basting occasionally with the red wine.

Add all the rice and toast the grains thoroughly with the rest of the ingredients for about 5 minutes. Add 3 ladlefuls of hot stock and stir gently until the rice has absorbed almost all the liquid. Then begin to add more stock, 1½ ladlefuls at a time, stirring constantly and making sure that the rice does not stick as it cooks.

After about 20 minutes, the rice should be tender but firm to the bite – but not chalky or over-soft. At this point, take the pan off the heat and stir in the remaining butter, the cheese and the parsley. Keep it fairly wet by adding a little bit more stock, then cover and leave to rest for about 4 minutes.

Serve on warmed individual plates or a large warmed platter, with extra cheese offered separately and plenty of robust red wine!

It is the marvellously sweet combination of flavours that makes this rich risotto a real winner. Together, the chicken livers, pancetta and peas make it a wonderfully comforting winter warmer.

Risotto with Chicken Livers and Peas

Risotto con Fegatini di Pollo e Pisellini

50 g/2 oz
unsalted butter

1 onion or 2 shallots,
very finely chopped

1 small carrot, peeled
and very finely
chopped

350 g/13 oz
Arborio rice

2 litres/8 cups
chicken stock, kept
simmering

1 tablespoon extra
virgin olive oil

100 g/4 oz chicken
livers, trimmed and
chopped

1/2 glass dry white wine

50 g/2 oz pancetta,
cubed

200 g/2 oz fresh or
frozen peas

50 g/2 oz freshly
grated Parmigiano
Reggiano

sea salt and freshly
milled black pepper

Serves 4

Melt 2 tablespoons of the butter in a large pan and fry the onion or shallots and carrot together until they are softened but not browned. Add the rice and stir into the vegetables until it is very hot and crackling.

Then add 3 ladlefuls of stock and stir until it has been absorbed by the rice. Continue adding more stock, 1–1 1/2 ladlefuls at a time, stirring continuously until the rice is tender but not soft.

Meanwhile, heat the olive oil in a small frying pan and fry the chicken livers until they are just browned: slightly pink in the middle and tender, not dark and leathery. Add the wine, then remove from the heat, season and set aside.

Melt 1 tablespoon of butter in another pan and fry the pancetta until it is browned, then add the peas. Stir, adding a little water to prevent sticking, and cover. Allow the peas to cook through, then remove from the heat, season and set aside.

Take the cooked risotto off the heat and stir in the chicken livers, peas, the remaining tablespoon of butter and half the Parmigiano Reggiano. Taste and adjust the seasoning, then cover and leave to rest for about 4 minutes. Serve on warmed individual plates or on a large serving dish, sprinkled with the remaining cheese.

There are lots of ingredients in this recipe, but they all work together beautifully. This really is a complete meal on one plate! This recipe is a Johannnesburg special, from Rhubarb in Sandton, that has been adapted in my own kitchen.

This is a good one for the children, as it is mild and gentle on the tastebuds and doesn't contain any unusual ingredients. Any good-quality ham is suitable, including Parma. For a much stronger flavour you could use ham bone stock, but watch the salt.

Risotto with Chicken, Broccoli, Butternut and Toasted Almonds

Risotto di Pollo, Broccoli, Zucca, e Mandorle Tostate

Risotto with Ham and Peas

Risotto con Prosciutto e Piselli

50 g/ 2 oz unsalted butter

1 onion, finely chopped

75 g/3 oz butternut squash, cubed

1 skinless chicken breast (portion), diced

100 g/4 oz broccoli, coarsely chopped

350 g/13 oz Arborio rice

1 glass dry white wine

up to 2 litres/8 cups chicken stock, kept simmering

a handful almonds, toasted and thinly sliced

50 g/2 oz freshly grated Parmigiano Reggiano, plus extra to serve

sea salt and freshly milled black pepper

Serves 4

Melt half the butter in a large pan, then add the onion, butternut squash, chicken and broccoli and cook until all the vegetables are softened, but the onion is not browned.

Add the rice and mix it with all the other ingredients, stirring until it is really hot and crackling. Add the wine and stir for a minute or two until the alcohol has evaporated and the liquid has been absorbed.

Next, start to add the stock, beginning with 3 ladlefuls. Stir and simmer until most of the stock has been absorbed. Lower the heat, then continue to add the stock 1–1½ ladlefuls at a time, stirring constantly and making sure the rice absorbs the liquid slowly.

When the rice is tender but firm to the bite, take the pan off the heat and stir in the remaining butter and the almonds. Season to taste and stir in the Parmigiano Reggiano. Cover and leave to rest for 4 minutes. Serve on a warmed platter with extra grated cheese offered separately.

40 g/1½ oz unsalted butter

1 small onion, finely chopped

350 g/13 oz Arborio rice

up to 2 litres/8 cups vegetable or chicken stock, kept simmering

150 g/5 oz cooked peas or petit pois

150 g/5 oz chopped, cooked ham

50 g/2 oz freshly grated Parmigiano Reggiano

1 tablespoon chopped fresh flat leaf parsley

sea salt and freshly milled black pepper

Serves 4

Melt half the butter in a large pan and fry the onion gently until soft but not browned. Add the rice and cook, stirring continuously, making sure that the mixture does not brown. When the rice is crackling hot, add the first 3 ladlefuls of hot stock. Stir thoroughly, until all the liquid has been absorbed, then add more stock, about 1½ ladlefuls at a time, waiting each time for the stock to be absorbed before adding another portion.

After 10 minutes, mix in the peas and three-quarters of the ham. Keep adding the stock, stirring the risotto thoroughly each time. When the rice is tender but firm to the bite, remove the risotto from the heat and add half the Parmigiano Reggiano and half the parsley and all the remaining butter.

Taste and season to taste with salt and pepper, then cover and rest the risotto for 4 minutes. Stir once more, then transfer onto a warmed serving dish and serve at once. Garnish with remaining cheese and parsley.

If you cannot find Luganega sausage, then opt for the same weight of other Italian sausages. Luganega is easy to spot because it is made in a continuous coil. Any other kind of raw Italian Sausage can be used instead.

Risotto with Italian Sausage

Risotto alla Luganega

75 g/3 oz unsalted butter

1 large onion, finely chopped

450 g (I lb) raw Italian Luganega sausage, skinned and crumbled

a handful of dried porcini mushrooms, soaked in tepid water for 20 minutes

1 tablespoon tomato puree

500 g/1lb 2oz Arborio rice

up to 2 litres/8 cups beef or chicken stock, kept simmering

50 g/2 oz freshly grated Parmigiano Reggiano, plus extra to serve

sea salt and freshly milled black pepper

Serves 6

Melt half the butter in a large pan and gently fry the onion with the sausage until the onion is soft and the sausage cooked through.

Drain the mushrooms and reserve the liquid. Chop the mushrooms coarsely and add to the pan. Stir and cook for a few minutes, basting with the strained liquid from the mushrooms. Add the tomato purée and stir to mix through. Cover and simmer for about 15 minutes, stirring occasionally and adding a little stock from time to time to prevent sticking.

Add the rice and stir thoroughly. When the rice has heated through, add the first ladleful of stock and stir again. Continue adding stock and stirring, making sure the rice absorbs all the liquid each time before adding in any more. Season to taste with salt and pepper.

When the risotto is creamy and the rice is tender but not soft, take the pan off the heat. Stir in the remaining butter and the Parmigiano Reggiano, then stir and cover. Leave to rest for 2 minutes, then stir again before transferring onto a warmed platter to serve. Serve immediately with extra Parmigiano Reggiano served separately at the table.

For this recipe you need typically Italian crumbly, peppery sausages with a very high meat content. While raw, they appear meaty and soft but become almost gritty when cooked. The two textures, soft mushrooms and chewy sausage make for an interesting texture. To improve the flavour of the dish, use strong, good-quality fresh mushrooms.

Risotto with Italian Sausage and Mushroom

Risotto con Salsiccia e Funghi

1 large onion, very finely chopped

4 large Italian sausages, skinned and crumbled

2 tablespoons extra virgin olive oil

2 handfuls mushrooms, peeled and coarsely chopped

350 g/13 oz Arborio rice

½ glass dry red wine

up to 2 litres/8 cups chicken or pork stock, kept simmering

50 g/2 oz unsalted butter

60 g/2½ oz freshly grated Parmigiano Reggiano

sea salt and freshly milled black pepper

a little chopped fresh flat leaf parsley, to garnish

Serves 4

In a large pan, gently fry the onion with the sausage in the olive oil until the onion is soft but not browned. Add the mushrooms and cook until they are soft.

Add the rice and mix with the other ingredients, stirring continuously until the rice is crackling hot. Add the red wine and stir for a further 2 minutes. Next, add about 3 ladlefuls of the stock, stirring continuously until the rice has absorbed all the liquid. Lower the heat then add the remaining stock a ladleful at a time, continuing to stir until all the liquid has been absorbed before adding more.

As soon as the rice is tender but firm to the bite, remove it from the heat and stir in the remaining butter and the 5 tablespoons of Parmigiano Reggiano. Taste and adjust the seasoning. Add a little more stock to loosen the risotto and cover the pan and leave to rest for 4 minutes. Transfer to a warmed platter or individual plates. Sprinkle with the parsley and serve with extra Parmigiano Reggiano offered separately.

The taste of pancetta is very distinctive and quite different from bacon. Fortunately it is widely available these days, so you really should not have any trouble finding it. If you are unlucky and cannot find it, the only possible substitute for this recipe is really top quality, green streaky (fatty) bacon.

Any white meat will work in this recipe so chicken, turkey, rabbit or veal are all fine. The 'white' in the recipe title actually refers to the fact that there is no tomato in the recipe, rather than the fact that the meat is white. This is one of the very rare risotto recipes which permits the addition of cream.

Risotto with Pancetta and Leeks

Risotto con Pancetta e Porri

3 tablespoons extra virgin olive oil

400 g/14 oz leeks, finely chopped

150 g/5 oz finely sliced pancetta, chopped

400 g/14 oz Arborio rice

up to 2 litres/8 cups chicken or vegetable stock, kept simmering

50 g/2 oz unsalted butter

50 g/2 oz freshly grated Parmigiano Reggiano

Finely sliced pancetta or bacon rashers

sea salt and freshly milled black pepper

Serves 4

Heat the oil in a large pan and fry the leeks and pancetta until the leeks are cooked through and soft.

Add the rice and stir thoroughly to coat in the oil. When the rice is crackling hot add the stock a ladleful at a time. Stir constantly until the liquid has been absorbed. Continue to add more stock until the risotto is tender but firm to the bite.

Remove the pan from the heat and stir in the butter and cheese. Adjust the seasoning, cover the pan and leave to rest for about 3 minutes. Stir again and transfer to a warmed platter or individual plates and serve at once, garnished with a few rashers of finely sliced pancetta, grilled until crispy.

Risotto with a White Ragu

Risotto al Ragu Bianco

75 g/3 oz unsalted butter

1 onion, chopped

1 celery stick, chopped

400 g/14 oz boned and cubed chicken, turkey or rabbit

juice and zest of ½ lemon

1 glass dry white wine

400 g/14 oz risotto rice

up to 2 litres/8 cups chicken stock, kept simmering

5 tablespoons single (light) cream

50 g/2 oz freshly grated Parmigiano Reggiano

2 teaspoons chopped fresh parsley

sea salt and freshly milled black pepper

Serves 4

Melt half the butter in a large pan and gently fry the onion and celery until they are soft. Add the meat to the pan and brown all over. Add the lemon zest and juice, stir again and then add the wine. Season and simmer everything together, basting with the hot stock if necessary, until the meat is tender.

Add the rice and stir thoroughly heating until the rice is crackling hot. Start adding the stock a ladleful at a time, stirring constantly, until all the liquid is absorbed. Continue to cook the rice in this way, making sure that the rice always absorbs the stock before you add more liquid.

When the risotto is tender and creamy, but the rice is firm to the bite, take the pan off the heat. Check the seasoning and stir in the remaining butter, the cream and the cheese. Stir thoroughly and cover. Leave to rest for 2–3 minutes, then transfer onto a warmed platter, sprinkle with the parsley and serve at once.

You need a rich ragu sauce for this risotto for it to be really outstanding. Allow yourself plenty time and make the ragu a day in advance so that the flavours have time to develop.

Risotto with Tomato Ragu

Risotto al Ragu col Pomodoro

4 tablespoons extra virgin olive oil

1 onion, chopped

1 carrot, chopped

1 celery stick, chopped

1 thick slice prosciutto crudo, chopped

250 g/9 oz minced beef or veal

1 glass dry red wine

400 g/14 oz thick passata (bottled strained tomatoes)

$\frac{1}{2}$ dried bay leaf

350g/13 oz risotto rice

up to 2 litres/8 cups chicken or beef stock, kept simmering

25 g/1 oz unsalted butter

50 g/2 oz freshly grated Parmigiano Reggiano

sea salt and freshly milled black pepper

Serves 4

First, make the ragu, preferably starting the day before. Heat the oil in a large pan and fry all the vegetables and the prosciutto until the vegetables are soft. Add the minced meat and the wine. Brown the meat and cook until the alcohol has evaporated. Then, add the passata and the bay leaf. Season to taste and cover. Simmer gently for about 2 hours or until the sauce is rich and dense with a bright orange rim.

If you are making the sauce in advance, remove the pan from the heat, cool then refrigerate until required. If not, continue from this point by adding the rice to the ragu. Stir until the sauce is becoming dry, then start to add the stock, stirring constantly and allowing the liquid to be absorbed before adding more. Continue to cook the rice in this way, ensuring that the stock is absorbed before adding more liquid.

When the risotto is creamy and the rice is tender but firm to the bite, remove the pan from the heat, discard the bay leaf and stir in the butter and cheese. Adjust seasoning then cover and rest for about 3 minutes before transferring to a warmed serving dish Serve with extra Parmigiano Reggiano offered separately.

The classic combination of eggs beaten to a creamy texture with freshly grated Parmesan and spiced up with black pepper, crisply fried pancetta cubes and a tiny hint of garlic are brought together in this risotto.

Risotto Carbonara

Risotto alla Carbonara

25 g/1 oz unsalted butter

1 garlic clove, finely chopped

1 small onion, finely chopped

200 g/7 oz cubed smoked pancetta

350 g/13 oz Arborio rice

up to 2 litres/8 cups chicken or pork stock, kept simmering

5 large egg yolks

100 g/4 oz freshly grated Parmigiano Reggiano or Grana Padano

1 tablespoon Mascarpone

sea salt and freshly milled black pepper

Serves 4

Melt half the butter in a large pan and fry the onion and half the pancetta until the onion is soft and cooked through but not browned.

Add the rice and toast the grains thoroughly without browning, making sure they are crackling hot before you add 3 ladlefuls of hot stock. Stir to allow the rice to absorb most of the liquid, and as soon as it starts to dry out, add another $1\frac{1}{4}$ ladlefuls of stock and continue to stir. Continue in this way until the rice is tender but firm to the bite.

Meanwhile, beat the egg yolks with the cheese, the Mascarpone and plenty of black pepper. Fry the remaining pancetta cubes in a small pan until crisp and brown. When the rice is ready, remove from the heat and add the remaining butter and the egg mixture. Mix together very thoroughly and taste to adjust the seasoning. Cover and leave to rest for about 4 minutes, then stir again and serve on warmed plates, topped with a scattering of the fried pancetta cubes.

The smoky taste of the Speck blends deliciously with the nutty flavour of the fontina as it melts through the rice. This risotto is very rich and filling, and needs a light red or a robust white wine to drink with it.

Risotto with Speck and Fontina

Risotto con Speck e Fontina

40 g/1½ oz unsalted butter

1 onion, finely chopped

150 g/5 oz finely chopped Speck

350 g/13 oz Carnaroli rice

1 glass dry white wine

up to 2 litres/8 cups chicken stock, kept simmering

200 g/7 oz Fontina, cubed

sea salt and freshly milled black pepper

Serves 4

Melt half the butter in a large pan and fry the onion gently with the Speck until the onion is soft and but not browned.

Add all the rice and mix with the other ingredients, toasting the grains until they are crackling hot. Now add the glass of white wine and stir continuously for about 1 minute as the alcohol evaporates and the liquid is absorbed. Add 3 ladlefuls of hot stock and keep stirring until all the liquid has been absorbed, then add another 1½ ladlefuls and stir again, keeping the heat quite low so the rice has time to absorb the liquid before it evaporates.

When the rice is tender but still firm to the bite, take it off the heat and add all the cheese and the remaining butter. Stir and taste, adding seasoning if required. Stir in one last ladleful of hot stock and cover the pan. Leave to rest for about 4 minutes, then transfer the risotto onto a warmed serving dish or individual plates and eat immediately.

If you like a creamy but light textured risotto with mild and comforting flavours then this is one for you. As always when there are very few and simple ingredients, make sure they are the very best. You can substitute the Speck with Prosciutto crudo if you prefer.

Risotto with Speck and Mascarpone

Risotto con Speck e Mascarpone

40 g/1½ oz unsalted butter

1 mild onion or small trimmed leek, finely chopped

½ dried bay leaf

200 g/7 oz Speck, cut into small strips

350 g/13 oz Arborio rice

2 litres/8 cups chicken, turkey or vegetable stock, kept simmering

3 tablespoons Mascarpone

50 g/2 oz freshly grated Parmigiano Reggiano

sea salt and freshly milled black pepper

Serves 4

Melt half the butter in a large pan and gently fry the onion or leek with the bay leaf and half the Speck (the fattier half) until the onion is soft but not browned.

Add the rice, and toast the grains for up to 5 minutes, stirring constantly to prevent it from browning. When the rice is crackling hot, add 3 ladlefuls of stock. Keep stirring until most of the stock has been absorbed by the rice. Lower the heat and continue to add the stock 1½ ladlefuls at a time, stirring constantly.

After about ten minutes, remove the bay leaf then continue to cook the risotto as before, adding stock and stirring until the rice has absorbed the liquid.

When the risotto is creamy and the rice tender but firm to the bite, remove the pan from the heat and stir in the remaining lean Speck, butter and Mascarpone, as well as half the Parmigiano Reggiano. Taste and season with salt and pepper then cover and leave to rest for 4 minutes. Transfer on to a warmed serving dish, dust with the remaining Parmigiano Reggiano and serve at once.

Sexy, Summery Recipes

Cheese, Herbs and Spices

Vegetables and Mushrooms

Fish and Meat

A real meal in itself, this is a wonderfully filling, brightly-coloured risotto that will feed many hungry people. You may not use all the vegetables, but once grilled and dressed you can use them on pasta, crostini or in a salad.

Risotto alla Parmigiana with Grilled Vegetables

Risotto alla Parmigiana con le Verdure alla Griglia

For the vegetables

2 courgettes (zucchini), sliced thinly lengthways

2 yellow or red (bell) peppers, sliced lengthways and seeded

1 aubergine (eggplant)

1 large onion, sliced across the centre into 8 thick rings

1 fennel bulb, sliced across the centre into 8 thick rings

4 tomatoes, sliced very thickly across the centre

200 ml/1 cup olive oil

2 garlic cloves, finely chopped

2 tablespoons chopped fresh flat leaf parsley

salt and freshly milled black pepper

extra oil, for serving

175 g/6 oz Parmigiano Reggiano shavings, to serve

For the risotto

40 g/1½ oz unsalted butter

1 onion, chopped finely

350 g/13 oz Arborio rice

1 glass dry white wine

up to 2 litres/8 cups rich chicken stock, kept simmering

60 g/2½ oz freshly grated Parmigiano Reggiano

sea salt and freshly milled black pepper

Serves 4

First, prepare the aubergine (eggplant) by slicing it lengthways, sprinkling with salt and leaving to stand in a colander under a weighted plate for an hour before rinsing and drying.

Next, cook the vegetables. Heat the grill (broiler) to medium. Brush all the vegetables with olive oil then grill (broil) in batches until they are just tender. As soon as the vegetables are cooked, and while they are still warm, arrange them in a wide, shallow bowl and sprinkle with the chopped garlic and parsley, and season with salt and pepper. When all the vegetables are in the bowl, sprinkle them with olive oil and set aside, keeping the vegetables warm.

Now make the risotto. Melt half the butter in a large pan and fry the onion gently until it is very soft but not coloured. Add the rice and toast the grains for about 5 minutes, then pour in the wine and stir for 1 minute until the alcohol has evaporated.

Add 3 ladlefuls of stock and stir until the rice has absorbed the liquid. Keeping the heat low, continue to add the stock, 1½ ladlefuls at a time, waiting each time for the grains to absorb the liquid before adding more.

When the rice is tender but still firm to the bite, take it off the heat and stir in the Parmigiano Reggiano and the remaining butter. Stir, taste and add salt and pepper if required. Cover and rest for about 4 minutes, then stir again and transfer onto a warmed platter. Arrange the warm, dressed vegetables on top of the risotto and scatter over the Pamigiano Reggiano shavings – then simply enjoy!

Serve with a green salad to follow.

I was given this recipe by a lady I met in a lift (elevator). She said she had eaten this risotto in a pub in Chester and that it had really stayed in her mind, so I thought I'd give it a go. We went up and down in the lift a few times while she explained it to me and I took copious notes.

I have no idea if this is anything like the original, but I like it very much. So I owe my thanks to the lady in the lift and the chef who cooked it for her, neither of whose names I know! It is situations like these which make life such fun – but embarrass my sons!

Risotto with Goat's Cheese and Spinach

Risotto con Formaggio di Capra e Spinaci

40 g/1½ oz unsalted butter

1 onion, finely chopped

350 g/13 oz Arborio rice

1 glass dry white wine

up to 2 litres/8 cups chicken or vegetable stock, kept simmering

3 handfuls fresh baby leaf spinach, washed and stalks removed

200 g/7 oz fresh semi-soft goat's cheese, cubed

50 g/2 oz freshly grated Parmigiano Reggiano

sea salt and freshly milled black pepper

Serves 4

Melt half the butter in a large pan and fry the onion very gently until it is soft but not browned.

Add the rice and toast the grains until they are crackling with the heat. Add the glass of wine and stir until the alcohol has evaporated, then add 3 ladlefuls of hot stock so that all the rice is submerged in the liquid. Stir continuously until the rice has absorbed most of the liquid

Reduce the heat and continue to add 1–1½ ladlefuls of stock at a time, stirring constantly until the liquid has been absorbed. After 10 minutes, add the prepared spinach and mix it in; then continue to cook the rice as before.

As soon as the rice is tender but still firm to the bite, take the pan off the heat and stir in the goat's cheese, the Parmigiano Reggiano and the seasoning, to taste. Add one final ladleful of stock, stir and cover. Leave the risotto to rest for 4 minutes, then transfer it to a warmed serving dish or individual plates to serve.

Basil can sometimes taste like liquorice if you don't treat it correctly or if the variety of basil is one that has this propensity. Remember not to cut basil with a knife or with scissors, as the metal will always bring the aniseed or liquorice flavour to the fore.

Risotto with Basil

Risotto al Basilico

3 cloves garlic, crushed

4 tablespoons extra virgin olive oil

2 handfuls fresh basil leaves, washed and torn into shreds

350 g/13 oz Arborio or Carnaroli rice

2 glasses dry white wine

up to 2 litres/8 cups vegetable or light chicken stock, kept simmering

50 g/2 oz freshly grated Parmigiano Reggiano

2 tablespoons pine kernels, toasted until golden brown and pungent

sea salt and freshly milled black pepper

a few sprigs of basil, to garnish

Serves 4

In a large pan, fry the garlic and basil very, very gently in the olive oil until the garlic is softened but not browned. Add the rice and toast the grains until they are crackling hot, then add the wine and stir for a couple of minutes until the alcohol has evaporated.

Then add 3 ladlefuls of the stock and stir until most of the liquid has been absorbed. Lower the heat and continue to add stock and stir the rice, waiting each time for the rice to absorb the liquid before adding more.

When the rice is tender but firm to the bite, take the pan off the heat and stir in the rest of the butter and almost all the Parmigiano Reggiano, reserving 1 tablespoon to finish the dish. Adjust the seasoning, and add a little more stock if the risotto is too dry, and cover. Leave to stand for about 4 minutes, then transfer onto a warmed serving dish. Garnish with the remaining cheese, the toasted pine kernels and the basil sprigs and serve at once.

If you ever make anything at all with nettles, make sure you are wearing a really good, stout pair of gloves before you even consider going out to start picking. Any nettle recipe, be it risotto, pasta, soup or salad, calls ideally for those lovely, fresh, tender, soft green sprigs which you will find in the spring. Should you opt to make this dish with older nettles, they must be stripped down to the stalk to remove their stings or the results will be a little chewy! Basically, you should treat nettles like most other green, leafy vegetables, if slightly more perilous to your tender skin!

Risotto with Nettles

Risotto all'Ortica

1 large, mild onion, finely chopped

1 large celery stick, finely chopped

75 g/3 oz unsalted butter

500 g/1 lb 2 oz freshly-picked nettles, washed, dried and finely chopped

400 g/14 oz Arborio rice

1 glass medium dry white wine or rosé wine

up to 2 litres/8 cups chicken or vegetable stock, kept simmering

75 g/3 oz freshly grated Parmigiano Reggiano, plus extra for serving

sea salt and freshly milled black pepper

Serves 4

Melt half the butter in a large pan and fry the onion and celery until soft. Add the nettles and stir, then cook for a few minutes until completely soft and tender, adding a little water if necessary to prevent sticking.

Add the rice and mix thoroughly until the grains are shiny, well coated and very hot. Pour in the wine and stir until the alcohol has evaporated. Add a little hot stock and stir until the rice has absorbed all the liquid, then add more. Stir, wait for the liquid to be absorbed, then add more stock. Continue in this way for about 20 minutes until the rice is creamy and tender but still firm in the centre of the grain.

Remove from the heat and stir in the remaining butter and the Parmigiano Reggiano. Season with salt and pepper then cover and leave to rest for about 3 minutes. Transfer to a warmed platter and serve immediately. Offer extra Parmigiano Reggiano separately at the table.

I adore the taste of rocket so much that I could not possibly leave it out of this collection of recipes! Be sure to let the rocket only wilt, but not actually cook, as this alters its flavour. Another rare recipe which allows a little cream!

Risotto with Rocket

Risotto con la Rucola

75 g/3 oz unsalted butter

1 onion, chopped

400 g/14 oz risotto rice

½ glass dry white wine

up to 2 litres/8 cups chicken stock, kept simmering

2 handfuls of rocket (arugula), washed, dried and coarsely chopped

3 tablespoons single (light) cream

60 g/2½ oz freshly grated Parmigiano Reggiano

sea salt and freshly milled black pepper

Serves 4

Melt half the butter in a large pan and fry the onion gently until soft, then add the rice and stir it thoroughly until it is opaque and sizzling hot.

Add the wine and allow the alcohol to evaporate for 1–2 minutes. Begin adding the stock 1 ladleful at a time, stirring constantly and making sure the rice absorbs all the liquid before adding any more. Gradually, as you stir in the stock, the risotto will become creamy and smooth.

When the rice is tender but still firm to the bite, add the rocket, cream and Parmigiano Reggiano. Adjust the seasoning, stir again and cover. Leave to rest for 2 minutes, then transfer onto a warmed platter and serve at once.

This is possibly my favourite risotto as it essentially encompasses my philosophy of food: less is more! In other words, use very few ingredients but make sure that they are all of the highest quality and that they are very simply cooked. You must use flat leaf parsley for this risotto. I have tried to make the same recipe with the curly variety, but with disappointing results.

Risotto with Parsley
Risotto di Prezzemolo

75 g/3 oz unsalted butter

1 onion, very finely chopped

400 g/14 oz Arborio rice

1 glass dry white wine (Pinot Grigio is my preference)

up to 2 litres/8 cups rich chicken stock, kept simmering

a very large bunch of fresh flat leaf parsley

75 g/3 oz freshly grated Parmigiano Reggiano

sea salt and freshly milled black pepper

Serves 4

First, prepare the parsley by washing and drying it. Cut off and discard the stalks and then finely chop the leaves. Set aside until needed.

Melt half the butter in a large pan and fry the onion gently until soft and translucent. Add the rice and heat in the butter and onion until it is shiny and very hot. Add the glass of wine and stir for 1 minute until the alcohol has evaporated.

Next, add the first ladleful of stock, stirring until the grains have absorbed the liquid. Continue to add the stock waiting for the liqud to be absorbed before adding more.

When the risotto is creamy and the rice is tender but still firm to the bite, season with salt and pepper; then take the pan off the heat. Stir in the rest of the butter, the prepared parsley and the cheese. Stir thoroughly and cover. Leave the risotto to rest for 2 minutes, then transfer onto a warmed platter and serve at once.

I like to make this risotto especially creamy and then, for contrast,
I finish it off with finely shredded fresh basil and a few toasted
pine kernels.

Risotto with Pesto

Risotto al Pesto

1 onion, finely chopped

1 garlic clove, finely chopped

4 tablespoons extra virgin olive oil

400 g/14 oz risotto rice

up to 2 litres/8 cups chicken or vegetable stock, kept simmering

$\frac{1}{2}$ jar (about 3 tablespoons) good-quality pesto

3 tablespoons double (heavy) cream or Mascarpone

50 g/2 oz freshly grated Parmigiano Reggiano

a handful of fresh basil leaves, torn into small shreds

a handful of pine kernels, lightly toasted

Serves 4

In a large pan, fry the onion and garlic gently in the olive oil until the onion is soft, then add the rice.

Raise the heat and stir in the rice, cooking until the grains are very hot. Then add the first ladleful of stock and stir until the rice has absorbed almost all the liquid. Continue to add the stock 1–1$\frac{1}{2}$ ladles at a time. Stir continuously and wait for each ladleful to be absorbed by the rice before adding more liquid.

When the risotto is velvety and the rice tender but still firm to the bite, stir in the pesto and heat through, adjusting the seasoning to taste. Remove the pan from the heat and stir in the cream or the Mascarpone and the Parmigiano Reggiano. Cover and leave to rest for 2–3 minutes, then stir once more and transfer to a warmed platter. Sprinkle with the basil and the pine kernels and serve at once.

This risotto brings together all the best flavours of summer. My son
Jamie, the budding new chef, is quite good at making this one for me.

Risotto with Wilted Rocket and Fresh Tomato

Risotto con la Rucola e Pomodoro Fresco

**3 tablespoons extra
virgin olive oil**

**2 garlic cloves, very
finely chopped**

**450 g/1 lb ripe, fresh,
sweet tomatoes,
seeded**

**350 g/13 oz
Arborio rice**

**up to 2 litres/8 cups
intensely-flavoured
vegetable stock, kept
simmering**

**4 handfuls of fresh
rocket (arugula),
washed and dried**

**50 g/2 oz freshly
grated Parmigiano
Reggiano**

**sea salt and freshly
milled black pepper**

Serves 4

Warm the oil in a large pan and fry the garlic very gently until it
releases its aroma. Add three-quarters of the tomatoes and stir
thoroughly, cooking until the tomatoes begin to fall apart.

Add the rice and heat it thoroughly all over, stirring frequently. After
about 5 minutes, add 3 ladlefuls of hot stock and stir until the rice has
absorbed almost all the liquid. Lower the heat and continue to add the
stock, $1\frac{1}{2}$ ladles at a time, only adding more stock when the rice has
absorbed the previous quantity of liquid.

Continue in this way until the risotto is creamy and the rice is tender
but still firm to the bite. Season to taste with salt and pepper, and add
the remaining tomatoes, 3 handfuls of the rocket and the cheese. Stir
thoroughly then cover and leave to rest for about 4 minutes. Transfer to
a warmed serving dish or individual plates and serve at once, sprinkled
with the remaining rocket leaves.

You need to use the smallest, freshest and most tender broad beans to make this risotto successfully. If the skins of the beans are not tender, then I am afraid you will have to blanch and then peel them before adding them to the risotto! Can also be made with borlotti beans, as pictured.

Risotto with Broad Beans and Pancetta

Risotto con le Fave e la Pancetta

1 onion, chopped finely

150 g/5 oz smoked pancetta, diced

3 tablespoons unsalted butter

350 g/13 oz Arborio rice

1 glass dry white wine

up to 2 litres/8 cups rich chicken stock, kept simmering

4 handfuls young broad (fava) beans (peeled if the skins are tough)

60 g/2½ oz freshly grated Parmigiano Reggiano

sea salt and freshly milled black pepper

Serves 4

Melt half the butter in a large pan and gently fry the onion and pancetta until the onion is very soft but not coloured.

Add the rice and cook, stirring for about 5 minutes or until the grains are crackling hot. Add the wine and stir for 1 minute, then add 3 ladlefuls of stock and stir thoroughly. Keeping the heat low, continue to stir and add stock, 1½ ladlefuls at a time, waiting each time for the rice to absorb the liquid before adding more.

After 10 minutes, add the broad beans and continue to cook the rice as before. As soon as the rice is tender but firm to the bite, take it off the heat and stir in the Parmigiano Reggiano and the remaining butter. Stir, taste and adjust the seasoning as required. Cover and leave to rest for about 4 minutes. Stir again and transfer the risotto onto a serving dish or warmed plates. Serve at once, with extra cheese offered separately.

I have suggested adding the aniseed liqueur only to heighten the liquorice flavour of the fennel. If you want less liquorice taste, leave out the aniseed liqueur. As an alternative, try a couple of tablespoons of Limoncello instead.

Risotto with Fennel

Risotto di Finocchi

500 g/1 lb 2 oz fennel bulbs

75 g/3 oz unsalted butter

1 onion, finely chopped

500 g/1 lb 2 oz Arborio rice

2–3 tablespoons dry aniseed liqueur (optional)

up to 2 litres/8 cups chicken or vegetable stock

75 g/3 oz freshly grated Parmigiano Reggiano

sea salt and freshly milled black pepper

Serves 4

Having established the sex of your fennel bulbs (the female bulb which is whiter and fatter, with smooth rounded buttocks, is considered far superior!), peel off all the hard external leaves and trim away all the green bits so you are left with tender, white fennel hearts. Slice the hearts thinly and evenly and fry in a large pan with half the butter and the onion.

Cook until the fennel is tender, then add the rice and stir until it has heated through. Add the liqueur, if using, and stir again. Season thoroughly and begin to add the stock gradually, 1–1½ ladlefuls at a time and stirring after each addition of stock so that the rice can absorb the liquid before more is added.

Continue to stir and add stock until the risotto is creamy and the rice is tender but firm to the bite. When you reach this stage, stir in the rest of the butter and the Parmigiano Regianno. Cover and remove from the heat. Leave the risotto to rest for about 2 minutes, then stir again before transferring it on to a warmed platter to serve.

The asparagus season is all too short, and whilst it is around it should be celebrated in as many ways as possible – including in a sumptuous risotto such as this one!

This is the most deliciously fresh-tasting combination of flavours I know. And they are all brought together against a backdrop of the creamy, nutty-tasting rice...perfect for a springtime or early summer lunch.

Risotto with Asparagus
Risotto con Asparagi

500 g/1 lb 2 oz fresh asparagus

75 g/3 oz unsalted butter

2 large shallots, peeled and chopped

500 g/1 lb 2 oz risotto rice

1.5 litres/6¼ cups chicken or vegetable stock, kept simmering

50 g/2 oz freshly grated Parmigiano Reggiano

1 tablespoon chopped fresh parsley

sea salt and freshly milled black pepper

Serves 6

In a deep pan, boil or steam the asparagus with a large pinch of salt for about 6 minutes or until the spears are just tender. Drain, reserving the cooking liquid, set aside to cool.

Melt half the butter in a large pan and fry the shallots for about 5 minutes until soft and transparent. Cut the asparagus into small pieces, leaving the tips intact. If the base of the asparagus spear is very tough, cut it off but scrape out the inside with a knife and add to the rest.

Add the rice and stir until it is very hot and shining. Then add the first ladleful of asparagus cooking liquid. Stir until the liquid has been absorbed, then add more, a ladleful at a time. When the asparagus cooking liquid is used, begin to add the stock. Continue in this way for about 20 minutes until the rice is tender but still firm to the bite.

Stir in the asparagus to heat through right at the end of the cooking time. Add the Parmigiano Reggiano and parsley and season to taste with pepper. Remove from the heat, cover and leave to stand for about 3 minutes. Transfer to a warmed serving platter and serve at once.

Risotto with Lettuce and Spring Onion
Risotto con le Cipolline e la Lattuga

40 g/1½ oz unsalted butter

8 spring onions (scallions), finely chopped

350 g/13 oz Arborio rice

1 small glass white wine

up to 2 litres/8 cups chicken or vegetable stock, kept simmering

1 head round (butterball) lettuce, washed, dried and coarsely shredded

50 g/2 oz freshly grated Parmigiano Reggiano

sea salt and freshly milled black pepper

Serves 4

Melt half the butter in a large pan and very gently and slowly fry the spring onions. When they are soft, add the rice and cook until rice is crackling and very hot. Then add the wine and stir until the alcohol has evaporated.

Next, start to add the stock, beginning with 3 ladlefuls so that the rice is completely covered in liquid. Stir thoroughly and allow the liquid to be absorbed. Lower the heat and continue to add stock 1–2 ladlefuls at a time, stirring constantly between each addition.

After about 20 minutes, the rice should be tender but firm to the bite. Remove the pan from the heat, stir in the lettuce and mix thoroughly until the leaves are wilted, then add the remaining butter, adjust the seasoning and stir in the Parmigiano Reggiano. Cover and leave to rest for about 4 minutes, then transfer onto a warmed serving dish or individual plates and eat at once.

One does not normally associate risotto with southern Italy, yet Sicily's proximity to North Africa gives the island an obvious link with rice as an ingredient. As the customs and traditions of Italian cuisine continue to evolve, to my mind there is no reason at all why Sicily should not also be allocated its own risotto recipe!

Risotto with a Sicilian Twist

Risotto alla Siciliana

3 tablespoons extra virgin olive oil

4 garlic cloves, finely chopped

$\frac{1}{2}$ dried red chilli, finely chopped

3 anchovies, rinsed, boned and chopped

1 teaspoon dried oregano

1 tablespoon salted capers, rinsed and finely chopped

2 tablespoons green olives, stoned (pitted) and chopped

1 tablespoon blanched almonds, chopped

350 g/13 oz Arborio rice

1 glass dry white wine

up to 2 litres/8 cups chicken or vegetable stock, kept simmering

2 tablespoons sun-dried tomato paste

40 g/1$\frac{1}{2}$ oz freshly grated Pecorino

sea salt and freshly milled black pepper

Serves 4

Warm the olive oil in a large pan and fry the garlic, chilli, anchovies, oregano, capers, olives and almonds for 3–4 minutes or until the garlic is soft. Add the rice and toast the grains thoroughly, mixing it thoroughly with the other ingredients and getting it really hot. Add the glass of wine and simmer for about a minute to allow the alcohol to evaporate; then add 3 ladlefuls of hot stock and stir until most of the liquid has been absorbed by the rice.

Lower the heat and continue to cook the rice, adding stock 1–1$\frac{1}{2}$ ladlefuls at a time and stirring while the rice absorbs each portion of stock. After 20 minutes, when the rice is tender but still firm to the bite, mix in the sun-dried tomato paste, adjust the seasoning and stir in the Pecorino. Pour in a little more stock so that the texture is velvety and not too dry, then cover and leave to rest for a few minutes. Transfer to a serving dish and eat at once.

A risotto that looks as good as it tastes! Make sure the fresh tomatoes are really packed with flavour before you begin. Add a little concentrated tomato purée if the flavour is too insipid, about ¾ teaspoon should suffice.

Scamorza is matured mozzarella that has been allowed to dry out. You can buy it either smoked or not, but for this recipe I think the smoked is much better as it increases the overall impact of the risotto. Tasty tomatoes are also important, otherwise they will get lost in the mix.

Risotto with Tomatoes

Risotto al Pomodoro

3 tablespoons extra virgin olive oil

2 garlic cloves, very finely chopped

$^1/_2$ teaspoon dried oregano

450 g/1 lb ripe, fresh, sweet tomatoes, washed and seeded

350 g/13 oz Arborio rice

up to 2 litres/8 cups intensely-flavoured vegetable stock, kept simmering

50 g/2 oz freshly grated Parmigiano Reggiano

sea salt and freshly milled black pepper

2 tablespoons chopped fresh flat leaf parsley, to garnish

Warm the oil in a large pan and then the garlic and the onion. Fry gently until the herbs release their aromas but do not colour. Add three-quarters of the tomatoes and stir thoroughly, cooking until the tomatoes begin to break down.

Add the rice and, stirring frequently, mix thoroughly with the tomatoes for about 5 minutes. Then add 3 ladlefuls of hot stock and stir while the rice absorbs the liquid. Lower the heat and continue to add the stock 1½ ladlefuls at a time, only adding more when the previous amount has been absorbed.

When the rice is tender but still firm to the bite, season to taste with salt and pepper. Add the remaining tomatoes and the Parmigiano Reggiano. Stir together thoroughly then cover and leave to rest for about 4 minutes. Transfer the risotto onto a warm serving dish or individual plates and serve at once, sprinkled with the chopped parsley.

Risotto with Tomatoes and Smoked Scamorza

Risotto con i Pomodori e la Scamorza Affumicata

4 tablespoons extra virgin olive oil

1 small onion, finely chopped

1 garlic clove, finely chopped

4 ripe tomatoes, peeled, seeded and coarsely chopped

1 tablespoon pine kernels

350 g/13 oz Arborio rice

up to 2 litres/8 cups chicken or vegetable stock, kept simmering

150 g/5 oz smoked Scamorza, finely diced

a small handful of fresh basil leaves, ripped into shreds

50 g/2 oz freshly grated Parmigiano Reggiano

sea salt and freshly milled black pepper

Serves 4

Warm the olive oil in a large pan and very gently fry the onion and garlic until softened but not coloured. Add the tomatoes and pine kernels and cook for a further 3 minutes, stirring.

Add the rice and heat, stirring constantly, until it is crackling hot but not browned. Then add the 3 ladlefuls of hot stock and stir until the rice has absorbed most of the liquid. Lower the heat and continue to add stock, about 1½ ladlefuls at a time, and stirring to allow the rice to absorb the liquid evenly. Continue to do this for about 20 minutes, waiting so that the rice has time to absorb the liquid before adding more stock.

When the rice is tender but still firm to the bite, remove the pan from the heat and add the Scamorza, the basil and half the Parmigiano Reggiano. Stir and season to taste before adding a final ladle of hot stock, stirring again and covering. Leave to rest for about 4 minutes, then transfer to a warmed platter and serve at once, sprinkled with the remaining cheese.

What makes this dish so delicious is the lovely sweet flavour of the roasted peppers and what makes it look so good is the brilliance of the colours. For these two reasons, I would recommend that you use either yellow or red peppers rather than green ones, which can turn bitter and lose their colour when cooked.

Risotto with Roasted Peppers
Risotto ai Peperoni Arrosto

3 juicy (bell) peppers washed and dried

75 g/3 oz unsalted butter

1 onion, finely chopped

1–2 garlic cloves, crushed

500 g/1 lb 2 oz risotto rice

up to 2 litres/8 cups vegetable or chicken stock, kept simmering

75 g/3 oz freshly grated Parmigiano Reggiano

sea salt and freshly milled black pepper

Serves 6

First, prepare the peppers. Heat the grill (broiler) to medium and grill (broil) the peppers all over until the outer skin is blackened. Remove the peppers from the heat and allow them to cool slightly before wrapping in clingfilm while they are still warm. Leave to stand for about 10 minutes, then unwrap. Rub off the charred outer skin under running cold water using a clean, new scouring pad. The surface flesh of the roasted, skinned peppers will probably be brownish in colour. Cut the pepper in half and remove all the inner seeds and membranes, then cut the flesh into thin strips and set them aside until needed.

Melt the butter in a large saucepan and fry the onion and garlic very gently until the onion is soft and transparent, then add the peppers. Stir gently over a low heat for about 5 minutes, then add the rice. Mix together until the rice is shiny and very hot. Then add the first ladleful of hot stock and stir until the rice has absorbed all the liquid.

Continue in this way, gradually adding the stock $1–1\frac{1}{2}$ ladlefuls at a time and stirring it in before adding more. When the rice is tender but still firm to the bite, season to taste and add the Parmigiano Reggiano. Remove the pan from the heat, cover and leave to stand for about 3 minutes before transferring to a warmed platter to serve.

This is an adaptation of one of my favourite pasta sauces, which is bright yellow with saffron and full of intriguing flavours that veer from the intensely fishy to the hot and spicy, all against the slightly peppery and clean-tasting foundation of the cauliflower.

A delicious risotto for the summer, full of flavour, light and perfect with a fresh green salad.

Risotto with Spicy Cauliflower

Risotto al Cavolfiore alla Siciliana

Risotto with Prawns and Garlic

Risotto con i Gamberetti all'Aglio

3 tablespoons extra virgin olive oil

3 garlic cloves, chopped

2 salted anchovies, boned, rinsed and finely chopped

1/4 dried red chilli pepper, finely chopped

1 large canned sardine, drained, boned and chopped

1/2 small cauliflower, broken into florets

1 tablespoon raisins, soaked in warm water until soft and swollen, drained

350 g/13 oz Arborio rice

1 small glass dry white wine

up to 2 litres/8 cups light vegetable stock, kept simmering

2 sachets of saffron powder or a large pinch of saffron threads

sea salt and freshly milled black pepper

Serves 4

If you are using saffron threads, soak them in water for 10 minutes, then strain and reserve the liquid, discarding the threads.

Warm the oil in a large pan and fry the garlic, anchovies, chilli and sardine for about 3 minutes or until the garlic is cooked and the anchovies have melted down. Add the cauliflower and the raisins and cook together gently until the cauliflower has softened. Then add the rice and stir for about 4 minutes until it is really hot, ensuring that none of the ingredients sticks.

Add the wine and stir again for a couple of minutes until the alcohol has evaporated. Then add 3 ladlefuls of the stock and stir while the rice absorbs the liquid. Then add more, 1 1/2 ladles at a time, waiting for the stock to be absorbed before adding more.

When the risotto is creamy and the rice is tender, take the risotto off the heat, taste and adjust seasoning, then mix in the saffron or the infusion from the threads. Mix everything together, cover and leave to rest for about 4 minutes, then transfer to a warmed serving dish and eat at once.

40 g/1 1/2 oz unsalted butter

3 garlic cloves, crushed

350 g/13 oz Arborio rice

1 glass dry white wine

250 g/9 oz cooked small prawns (shrimp)

up to 2 litres/8 cups full-flavoured fish stock, kept simmering

3 tablespoons chopped fresh flat leaf parsley

sea salt and freshly milled black pepper

3 tablespoons olive oil

1/2 garlic clove, finely chopped

4 large raw prawns (shrimp)

Serves 4

Melt half the butter in a large pan and very gently fry the garlic for about 3 minutes, taking care not to let it brown.

Then add rice and toast the grains until crackling hot. Add the wine and stir for 1 minute until the alcohol has evaporated, then add the small prawns and stir again. Begin to add the stock. Pour in 3 ladles and stir gently until most of the liquid has been absorbed. Then lower the heat and continue to cook the rice by adding 1 1/2 ladlefuls at a time, waiting for the rice to absorb the liquid each time before adding more.

When the rice is tender but still firm to the bite, take the risotto off the heat and stir in the parsley and seasoning. Add one more ladle of stock then cover and leave to rest for about 4 minutes.

While the risotto is resting, make the garnish. Heat the oil in a wide, shallow pan and gently fry the chopped garlic for about 1 minute. Add the large prawns and fry briefly on either side for about 2 minutes, or until pink and cooked through.

Serve on warmed plates, with a large prawn sitting jauntily on top of each portion.

With a wonderfully Mediterranean flavour, this is powerful risotto that really packs a punch. It's an ideal dish for warm summer evening dinners and al fresco lunches. Or when the grey winter makes it feel like summer will never come back, this risotto will remind you of blue skies and sunny days.

Risotto with Aubergines, Sun-dried Tomatoes and Pine Kernels

Risotto con le Melanzane, i Pomodori Secchi e i Pinoli

1 aubergine (eggplant), peeled and cubed

2 garlic cloves, finely chopped

1 salted anchovy, rinsed, dried and chopped

6 sun-dried tomatoes, sliced into strips

2 tablespoons pine kernels

3 tablespoons extra virgin olive oil

350 g/13 oz Arborio rice

up to 2 litres/8 cups vegetable stock

50 g/2 oz freshly grated Pecorino

a large handful chopped fresh flat leaf parsley

a handful of basil leaves, ripped into small pieces

sea salt and freshly milled black pepper

Serves 4

Place the cubed aubergine in a colander, sprinkle generously with salt and place a plate over the aubergine so it is pressing down on the cubed flesh. Put a heavy tin on the plate and place the colander in the sink so that the bitter juices can drain out of the aubergine. This should take about 30 minutes. When the aubergine has purged itself, rinse it thoroughly and dry it with paper towels.

Fry the garlic, anchovy, sun-dried tomatoes, pine kernels and aubergine together in the olive oil in a large pan, stirring constantly, until the anchovy has melted down completely. Then add the rice and stir to coat it in the other ingredients. When the rice is crackling hot, add 3 ladlefuls of the stock and mix until the liquid has been almost completely absorbed by the rice. Reduce the heat slightly and continue to add the stock a ladleful at a time, stirring while the liquid is absorbed and only adding more after the previous ladleful has been absorbed by the rice.

When the rice is tender but firm to the bite – this should take about 20 minutes – remove the pan from the heat and add the Pecorino, seasoning and the herbs. Leave to stand, covered, for 4 minutes, stir again and serve at once on warmed plates or on a serving dish.

Passata is a creamy tomato concoction made by puréeing skinned, seeded, tomatoes. It is available at most supermarkets and good grocers and is sold either in glass bottles or in cartons. It is very convenient as it cooks very quickly and gives a smooth, velvety consistency.

Risotto with Mushrooms and Tomatoes

Risotto di Funghi al Pomodoro

75 g/3 oz unsalted butter

1 onion, chopped

2 garlic cloves, finely chopped

1 tablespoon finely chopped fresh rosemary leaves

200 g/7 oz passata (bottled strained tomatoes)

1 teaspoon tomato puree

1 glass dry white wine

200 g/7 oz assorted fresh mushrooms

500 g/1 lb 2 oz Arborio rice

up to 2 litres/8 cups chicken or vegetable stock, kept simmering

sea salt and freshly milled black pepper

freshly grated Parmigiano Reggiano, to serve

Serves 4 to 6

Melt half the butter in a large pan and gently fry the onion and garlic until just soft. Then add the rosemary and the passata and mix together thoroughly before adding the tomato purée, wine and the mushrooms.

When the mushrooms have cooked down a little, add the rice and stir. Cook the grains until they are very hot and look opaque, then pour in the first ladleful of stock and stir until the liquid has been absorbed by the rice. Continue to cook the rice in this way, adding stock and stirring while the rice absorbs the liquid.

When the risotto is creamy and smooth, and the rice is tender but firm to the bite, remove the pan from the heat and stir in the remaining butter. Cover and rest for 1 minute, then transfer the risotto onto a warmed platter and serve at once. Offer the Parmigiano Reggiano separately at the table.

This combination of flavours is a classic of Roman cuisine, usually served as a topping on crostini or with pasta. It works very well with risotto, as the sweet nutty flavour of the rice offsets the smoky taste of the cheese and the sting of the anchovy particularly well.

Risotto with Anchovy and Scamorza

Risotto con l'Acciuga e la Scamorza

3 garlic cloves, crushed

1 tablespoon anchovy paste

4 tablespoons olive oil

350 g/13 oz Arborio rice

1 glass dry white wine

up to 2 litres/8 cups vegetable stock, kept simmering

200 g/7 oz smoked Scamorza, cubed

2 tablespoons chopped fresh flat leaf parsley

sea salt and freshly milled black pepper

Serves 4

In a large pan set over a low heat, melt the anchovy paste into the oil and garlic for about 4 minutes, then add the rice. Cook the grains thoroughly for about 8 minutes until very hot. Next, add the wine and stir for 2 minutes until the alcohol has evaporated.

Pour 3 ladlefuls of stock in to the pan and stir gently until the rice has absorbed most of the liquid. Turn down the heat and continue to add stock $1\frac{1}{2}$–2 ladlefuls at a time, stirring between each addition.

Continue in this way until the rice is tender firm to the bite. Then take the pan off the heat and stir in the cubed Scamorza. Add a little more stock and season with salt and pepper. Finally, stir through the parsley and cover. Leave to rest for about 4 minutes, then stir again and transfer onto a warmed platter or individual plates to serve.

This risotto is like a bit like a puttanesca sauce, full of punchy, sunny, hot flavours. Plenty of salad and cold white wine is required to go with this one!

Risotto with Anchovies, Capers and Olives

Risotto con Acciughe, Capperi e Olive

3 garlic cloves, crushed

a pinch of dried red chilli, chopped

2 salted anchovies, rinsed, boned and coarsely chopped

2 tablespoons salted capers, rinsed and finely chopped

5 tablespoons green olives, stoned (pitted) and coarsely chopped

1 tablespoon black olive pâté

4 tablespoons extra virgin olive oil

$\frac{1}{2}$ teaspoon dried oregano

350 g/13 oz Arborio rice

2 glasses dry white wine

up to 2 litres/8 cups strong vegetable stock or light fish stock, kept simmering

1 tablespoon tomato purée, diluted in $\frac{1}{2}$ glass warm water

sea salt

3 tablespoons chopped fresh flat leaf parsley

Serves 4

Put the garlic, chilli, anchovies, capers, olives, olive pâté, olive oil and oregano into a large pan and fry gently for about 5 minutes, stirring continuously. Add the rice and toast the grains for a few minutes until the rice is crackling hot, then add the wine and stir for about 3 minutes or until the alcohol has evaporated.

Lower the heat and start to add the hot stock, about $1\frac{1}{2}$–2 ladlefuls at a time, stirring thoroughly between each addition and always waiting for the rice to absorb the liquid before adding more.

As soon as the rice is tender but still firm to the bite, remove it from the heat and stir in the tomato purée diluted in the warm water. Adjust the seasoning and stir in the parsley. Cover and leave to rest for about 4 minutes, then stir once more before serving on a warmed platter or in warm bowls.

In this risotto, the combination of fish and courgettes gives a very distinctive overall taste. If you have some, you can also add courgette blossoms to the risotto for extra colour and flavour. Light yet nourishing, this fresh-tasting, creamy risotto makes a delicious summer lunch.

Risotto with Creamy Fish and Courgettes

Risotto al Pesce con le Zucchine

40 g/1¹/₂ oz unsalted butter

1 red onion, very finely chopped

1 garlic clove, very finely chopped

2 medium-sized courgettes (zucchini), cut into very small cubes

350 g/13 oz Vialone Nano rice

up to 2 litres/8 cups fish stock, kept simmering

200 g/7 oz white fish fillets, poached in milk and boned (see p. 52)

60 g/2¹/₂ oz small cooked peeled prawns (shrimp)

2 tablespoons finely chopped fresh flat leaf parsley

sea salt and freshly milled black pepper

Serves 4

Melt half the butter in a large pan, then add the onion and the garlic with the courgettes and fry until the onion is softened but not browned and the courgette is also beginning to soften.

Add the rice and stir until crackling hot, then add 3 ladlefuls of the stock. Stir until the rice has absorbed most of the liquid. Continue to add more stock 1¹/₂–2 ladlefuls at a time, stirring continuously and only adding more stock when the rice has absorbed the liquid.

After about 10 minutes, strain the fish and add its cooking milk to the risotto. Flake the fish and add that to the pan as well. Continue to cook the risotto as before until the rice is tender but still firm to the bite. Remove the pan from the heat and stir in the prawns, the remaining butter, the parsley and seasoning, to taste. Add a final generous ladle of fish stock, then cover and leave to rest for about 4 minutes. Stir once more before transferring onto a warmed platter or individual plates and serving.

A very fishy, summery risotto that is especially delicious when the olives are plump, juicy and very tasty. Make sure that you use tuna that has been canned in olive oil.

Risotto with Olives and Tuna

Risotto con le Olive e il Tonno

4 tablespoons extra virgin olive oil

4 cloves garlic, finely chopped

a large handful stoned (pitted) green or black olives, coarsely chopped

1 tablespoon black olive paste

350 g/13 oz Arborio rice

up to 2 litres/8 cups light fish or vegetable stock, kept simmering

250 g/9 oz best-quality canned tuna in olive oil, drained and coarsely flaked

a handful of chopped fresh flat leaf parsley

sea salt and freshly milled black pepper

whole olives, to garnish

Serves 4

Warm 3 tablespoons of the oil in a large pan and fry the garlic, olives and olive paste until the garlic is cooked but not browned.

Add the rice and toast the grains for about 5 minutes or until they are crackling hot. Then add 3 ladlefuls of stock and stir until the rice has absorbed most of the liquid. Continue to add the stock $1\frac{1}{2}$ ladlefuls at a time, stirring while the rice absorbs the liquid and only adding more stock when the previous quantity has been absorbed.

As soon as the risotto is creamy and the rice is tender but firm to the bite, take the risotto off the heat and stir in the tuna. Taste and adjust the seasoning before adding the parsley and the remaining tablespoon of oil. Cover and leave to stand for about 4 minutes, then stir again. Serve at once on warmed plates or a warmed serving platter, garnished with a few whole olives.

Because it was so complicated to make, I have had to rethink this recipe completely over the years. I dedicate this new, revised and much simper version to anyone who tackled the earlier – and more complicated – recipe! That said, it is a wonderful and sophisticated risotto that deserves every bit of effort needed to make it.

Risotto with Prawns (Revisited)

Risotto con i Gamberetti

150 g/5 oz unsalted butter

1 medium onion, roughly chopped

1 carrot, roughly chopped

6 fresh parsley stalks, roughly chopped

$\frac{1}{2}$ bay leaf

500 g/1 lb 2 oz fresh raw prawns (shrimp)

$\frac{1}{2}$ glass brandy

350 g/13 oz Carnaroli rice

2 glasses dry white wine

up to 2 litres/8 cups fish stock, kept simmering

Serves 4

First, cook the prawns and make a thick fish paste. Melt 3 tablespoons of butter in a pan and fry half the onion, the carrot, the parsley and the half bay leaf. When the vegetables are all soft, add the prawns and cook them quickly, basting with the brandy until they are cooked. Remove the pan from the heat and wait until the prawns are cool enough to handle.

Once they have cooled slightly, remove the prawns from the pan. Peel each prawn, keeping both the head and tail shells and the meat from the crustaceans. Set aside the peeled prawns. Gather together all the head and tail shells and place them in a food processor along with the softened vegetables. Blend until they are completely smooth.

Very slowly melt 125 g/4 oz of the butter in a saucepan. Add the prawn shell and vegetables puree and mix together to form a thick paste. Add about 1 ladleful of stock and stir thoroughly, then strain and set aside.

Melt the remaining butter in a large pan and fry the onion until it is soft and transparent. Add the rice and stir until crackling hot, then pour in the wine and stir until it has evaporated. Then begin to add the stock 1-1$\frac{1}{2}$ ladlefuls at a time waiting for the rice to absorb the liquid before adding more.

Continue in this way until the rice is tender but still firm to the bite and the risotto creamy. Adjust the seasoning and remove the pan from the heat; stir in the strained prawn concentrate and the cooked, peeled prawns. Mix together with one more ladleful of stock and cover. Leave to rest for 4 minutes, then stir again and serve at once on a warmed platter.

In some risotto recipes, the ingredients are so special that the rice is almost incidental, whereas in others it is the rice itself that is crucial. This is all part of the magic of risotto. In this dish, the rice is a kind of glue that holds all the other ingredients together. The finished result is sensational and definitely one of my favourites!

Risotto with Squid, Mussels and Tomato

Risotto con i Totani e le Cozze al Pomodoro

99

For the mussels

about 1 kg/2 lb 4 oz fresh, scrubbed mussels

a handful of parsley or parsley stalks

½ leek or onion, thickly sliced

2 glasses dry white wine

peel of 1 thick-skinned lemon (with no pith on peel)

For the squid

4 tablespoons olive oil

1 garlic clove, crushed

4 medium-sized squid, cleaned and cut into strips

1 glass dry white wine

6 tablespoons passata (bottled strained tomatoes)

For the risotto

4 tablespoons extra virgin olive oil

2 garlic cloves, lightly crushed

4 tomatoes, peeled and seeded, then chopped very coarsely

300 g/11 oz Vialone Nano rice

1 litre/4 cups fish stock, kept simmering

3 tablespoons chopped fresh flat leaf parsley

sea salt and freshly milled black pepper

Serves 4

Put the cleaned mussels into a large pot with the parsley, leek, white wine, the whole peeled lemon and half the peel (making sure there is no white pith on the rind). Season with salt and pepper then cover and steam for about 8 minutes. Take the pan off the heat, remove lid and leave to cool.

Meanwhile, wash and dry the squid. Heat the oil in a shallow pan and gently cook the garlic until it begins to release its pungent aromas, then remove the garlic and discard it, and add the squid to the pan. Stir for a 2–3 minutes, then add the wine. Allow the alcohol to evaporate for 1 minute, then add the passata. Stir and turn down the heat. Simmer gently for about 20 minutes or until the squid is soft. Season and set aside.

Remove all the opened mussels from the first pan and strain the liquid through a sieve and reserve. Discard any mussels that have not opened. Remove the mussels from their shells and reserve, keeping about 8 mussels in their shells as a garnish. Chop half the remaining pithless peel into small dice.

Now begin making the risotto. Heat the 4 tablespoons of olive oil in a pan with the crushed garlic. As soon as the garlic begins to release its aroma, remove it from the pan and discard. Add the tomatoes, rice and diced lemon peel to the pan; stir until the rice is crackling hot then add the reserved mussel liquid. Allow this to be absorbed by the rice, then continue to cook the risotto as normal, adding 1–1½ ladlefuls of hot fish stock at a time, waiting for the rice to absorb the liquid before adding in more.

Continue in this way until the rice is tender but not mushy but still firm to the bite. Stir in the squid, the reserved mussels, one more ladleful of stock and mix together thoroughly. Remove the pan from the heat, adjust the seasoning and stir in the chopped parsley. Leave to rest for about 3 minutes, then transfer to a warmed serving dish, garnish with the reserved mussels in their shells and serve at once.

This is always a favourite with children. It is a really simple, sweet and nourishing risotto with a slightly Chinese taste to it...If the children you cook for are anything like the ones I know, you will need to be especially careful about making sure the onion absolutely vanishes into the background and they aren't aware it is even there! Omit the parsley if any green at all is unacceptable!

Risotto with Chicken and Sweetcorn

Risotto al Pollo Con il Mais

40 g/1½ oz
unsalted butter

1 small onion, very
finely chopped

4 chicken thighs,
skinned, boned and
coarsely chopped

350 g/13 oz
Arborio rice

up to 2 litres/8 cups
strong chicken stock,
kept simmering

6 tablespoons
sweetcorn kernels,
canned, frozen or
fresh

50 g/2 oz freshly
grated Parmigiano
Reggiano

2 tablespoons
chopped fresh flat leaf
parsley

sea salt

Serves 4

Over a low heat, melt half the butter in a large pan and brown the chicken pieces on all sides. Lower the heat then add the onion and cook very slowly until it is softened but not browned. Add the rice and toast the grains for about 5 minutes, stirring constantly; then add 3 ladlefuls of stock. Stir until most of the liquid has been absorbed by the rice, then add more stock, 1½ ladlefuls at a time, and stir again until absorbed.

Continue to stir and add stock for 10 minutes, then stir in the corn and continue to cook as before until the rice is tender but still firm to the bite. Take the pan off the heat and stir in the remaining butter, the cheese and seasoning to taste. Mix in the parsley and one last ladle of stock and cover. Leave to rest for about 4 minutes, then serve with extra cheese offered at the table.

Rabbit is a delicious and much underestimated meat, so it is a shame that many people's sentimental feelings get in the way of them trying this cheap and readily available delicacy. This cooking method for the rabbit originates in Tuscany, where I come from. Here, they grow a special olive just for cooking with rabbit. In the absence of *olive per il coniglio* use small, sweet, slightly wrinkled olives with a bittersweet flavour. Do not use the rabbit carcass to make the stock as the result will be far too sickly sweet.

Risotto with Rabbit and Olives

Risotto al Coniglio con le Olive

4 tablespoons extra virgin olive oil

1 onion, chopped

1 celery stick, chopped

a handful of fresh flat leaf parsley, chopped

4 rashers of pancetta (or 4 slices of prosciutto crudo), chopped

1 rabbit (with a whole weight of about 2 kg/ 4 lb 6 oz), boned and cut in to 2.5 cm/ 1 in cubes

2 tablespoons tomato purée

1 glass dry red wine

about 18–20 pitted (stoned) black olives, coarsely chopped

a pinch of dried oregano

400 g/14 oz risotto rice

up to 2 litres/8 cups chicken or vegetable stock, kept simmering

sea salt and freshly milled black pepper

Serves 4

Heat the oil in a large pan and fry the onion, celery, parsley and the Pancetta until the onion is soft. Add the rabbit and brown all over. Mix the tomato purée with the wine and pour into the pan, then add the olives and the oregano. Season and stir, then cover and simmer for about 1½ hours, or until the rabbit is really tender and the meat is beginning to fall apart. Keep the mixture moist by occasionally adding a little stock or wine.

When the rabbit is cooked, pour the rice into the pan and stir to coat all the grains with the rabbit stew for about 5 minutes. Then begin to add the stock, a ladleful at a time, stirring constantly and allowing the liquid to be absorbed by the rice before adding more. Continue to cook the rice in this way until the risotto is creamy and the rice is tender but still firm to the bite. Remove the pan from the heat. Adjust the seasoning, then transfer onto a warmed platter to serve. Offer grated Parmigiano Reggiano separately at the table.

Dinner Party Recipes

Cheese, Herbs and Spices

Vegetables and Mushrooms

Fish and Meat

The size of the truffle you use is entirely up to you – or your finances! And maybe whether you are lucky enough to enjoy the bounty of nature and can find them wild. If you can't find a fresh black truffle (which are only available in late autumn and early winter) don't be tempted to use truffle oil, which has never been near a truffle, but use a good truffle butter instead, stirred through at the last moment.

Risotto with Black Truffle

Risotto al Tartufo Nero

40 g/1½ oz unsalted butter

1 onion, peeled and chopped finely

350 g/13 oz Carnaroli rice

1 large glass dry white wine

up to 2 litres/8 cups rich chicken stock, kept simmering

60 g/2½ oz freshly grated Parmigiano Reggiano

1 black truffle, cleaned and ready to shave

sea salt and freshly milled black pepper

Serves 4

Melt half the butter in a large pan and fry the onion gently until very soft but not coloured. Add the rice and thoroughly toast the grains for about 5 minutes until crackling hot.

Add the wine and stir for 1 minute, then add 3 ladlefuls of stock and stir until it has been absorbed by the rice. Reduce the heat to low and continue to add the stock a ladleful at a time, stirring while the stock is being absorbed by the rice. Continue in this way until the rice is tender but still firm to the bite.

Remove the pan from the heat and stir in the Parmigiano Reggiano and the remaining butter. Stir, taste and add salt and pepper as required. Cover and rest for about 4 minutes, then stir again and transfer on to 4 plates. Shave as much or as little of the black truffle over the steaming risotto as you want, and indulge yourself!

This risotto is seriously creamy and is another one which belongs to my son Jamie's repertoire of favourites.

Risotto with Mascarpone and Porcini Mushrooms

Risotto al Mascarpone con il Funghi Porcini

2 shallots finely chopped

40 g/1½ oz unsalted butter

200 g/7 oz fresh porcini mushrooms, finely sliced or 100 g/2 oz dried porcini

2 garlic cloves, finely chopped

350 g/13 oz Carnaroli rice

1 small glass dry white wine

2 litres/8 cups chicken or vegetable stock, kept simmering

4 tablespoons Mascarpone

50 g/2 oz freshly grated Parmigiano Reggiano

sea salt and freshly milled black pepper

Serves 4

If using dried porcini, soak them overnight in warm water, then drain through a sieve lined with kitchen paper, taking care to reserve the soaking water.

Melt half the butter in a large pan and fry the shallots with the mushrooms and the garlic, stirring frequently, until all the ingredients are cooked through.

Add the rice and toast thoroughly until sizzling hot. After about 3–4 minutes, add the wine and stir for a further minute, then add 2 ladlefuls of stock and the reserved mushroom liquid (If using fresh porcini, add 3 ladlefuls of hot stock.) Stir until most of the liquid has been absorbed by the rice. Lower the heat, adding the stock gradually and stirring until the rice has absorbed each addition of liquid.

When the rice is tender but firm to the bite, take it off the heat. Stir in the remaining butter, the Mascarpone and 3 tablespoons of the Parmigiano Reggiano; taste and season then add a little more stock and cover. Leave to rest for 4 minutes. Stir once more before transferring to a warm dish to serve sprinkled lightly with the last of the Parmigiano Reggiano.

This is a very unusual risotto, one that is sweet but spicily hot at the same time. I like to serve it at late night parties, when palates are a little jaded and need perking up, and appetites are waning slightly, but still on the peckish side!

Risotto with Mascarpone and Mustard Fruits

Risotto con il Mascarpone e la Mostarda di Frutta

An extremely unusual combination of flavours that is most suitable for the adventurous at Christmas time!

Risotto with Mustard Fruits, Chestnuts, and Amaretti Biscuits

Risotto con Mostarda di Frutta, Castagne e Amaretti

---

40 g/1½ oz unsalted butter

1 small shallot, very finely chopped

350 g/13 oz Carnaroli rice

1 glass dry white wine

up to 2 litres/8 cups very light vegetable stock, kept simmering

40 g/1½ oz Parmigiano Reggiano

¼ teaspoon freshly grated nutmeg

3 tablespoons Mascarpone

3–4 tablespoons mixed mustard fruits and their syrup, coarsely chopped

sea salt and freshly milled black pepper

Serves 4

Melt the butter in a large pan and fry the shallot gently until soft. Add the rice and turn it in the butter and shallot until the grains are toasted and crackling hot. Pour in the wine and cook for 1–2 minutes until the alcohol has evaporated, then add 3 ladlefuls of stock and stir again until the rice has absorbed most of the liquid.

Lower the heat and continue to cook the rice by adding the stock 1–2 ladlefuls at a time, stirring continuously and waiting to add more liquid only after the previous quantity has been absorbed.

When the grains are tender, but still firm to the bite. Take the risotto off the heat and stir in the Parmigiano Reggiano, nutmeg, Mascarpone and a final half ladleful of stock. Mix thoroughly and adjust the seasoning, then cover.

Leave to rest for about 4 minutes, then stir in about half the mustard fruits and half the syrup. Transfer onto a warmed platter or individual plates and arrange the remaining chopped fruits in the centre. Drizzle over the rest of the syrup and serve at once.

---

1 small onion, chopped very finely

40 g/1½ oz unsalted butter

350 g/13 oz Carnaroli rice

up to 2 litres/8 cups chicken or turkey stock, kept simmering

12 cooked chestnuts, peeled and coarsely chopped

6 amaretti biscuits, crumbled coarsely

2–3 tablespoons chopped mustard fruits and syrup

25 g/1 oz freshly grated Parmigiano Reggiano (optional)

sea salt and freshly milled black pepper

To garnish

1–2 tablespoons chopped fresh flat leaf parsley

1 tablespoon mustard fruits, drained and chopped

Serves 4

Melt half the butter in a large pan and fry the onion until the onion is softened but not browned. Add the rice and toast the grains thoroughly for about 5 minutes, stirring constantly to prevent browning.

When the rice is crackling hot, add about 3 ladlefuls of stock and stir through. Add the chestnuts and stir again, then continue to add stock and stir, adding more liquid only when the previous quantity has been absorbed. After about 10 minutes, add the crumbled amaretti and stir again. Continue to add the stock, as before, until the rice is cooked when it should be tender but firm to the bite.

Remove the pan from the heat and add a further ladleful of stock, the remaining butter, the mustard fruits and their syrup and the cheese, if using. Cover and rest for 4 minutes, then stir again and transfer to a warmed platter or onto individual warmed plates. Garnish with a sprinkling of chopped flat leaf parsley and a little spoonful of mustard fruits and serve at once.

This is a simple and traditional Piemontese recipe. It is based on a very plain risotto made with onion, butter, stock and Parmesan. Make sure you have a good bottle of Barolo on the table so that when you are ready to eat, you can scoop out a hollow in the centre of each portion and fill it with the wine. The combination of the hot risotto and the slightly warmed Barolo makes it fantastic... delicious!

Artichokes are without question my favourite vegetable and, although all this seems like a lot of work, the end results are so delicious you'll know it was all worth it!

Risotto alla Parmigiana with Barolo

Risotto alla Parmigiana con il Barolo

Risotto with Artichokes

Risotto ai Carciofi

1 onion, finely chopped

40 g/1½ oz unsalted butter

350 g/13 oz Arborio rice

1 glass dry white wine

up to 2 litres/8 cups rich chicken stock, kept hot

60 g/2½ oz freshly grated Parmigiano Reggiano

1 bottle of good Barolo wine or another full bodied Italian red wine e.g. Amarone, Nebbiolo, Dolcetto or vintage Chianti

sea salt and freshly milled black pepper

Serves 4

Melt half the butter in a large pan and fry the onion gently until very soft but not coloured. Add the rice and toast the grains in the butter and onions for about 5 minutes.

When the rice is very hot, add the wine and stir for 1 minute, then add 3 ladlefuls of stock and stir until the rice has absorbed most of the liquid. Reduce the heat and continue to stir and add stock, 1½ ladlefuls at a time, waiting each time for the liquid to be absorbed before adding more liquid.

As soon as the rice is tender but still firm to the bite, take it off the heat and stir in the Parmigiano Reggiano and the remaining butter. Stir, taste and season as required. Cover and leave to rest for about 4 minutes, then stir again and transfer onto 4 warmed plates. Serve with the Barolo that can be poured into a central hollow in the risotto, and with extra cheese offered separately.

8 large, fresh globe artichokes

1 lemon, quartered

75 g/3 oz unsalted butter

1 small onion, finely chopped

75 g/3 oz prosciutto crudo, chopped finely

a handful of fresh flat leaf parsley, finely chopped

1 glass dry white wine

400 g/14 oz Arborio rice

1.2 litres/5 cups chicken or vegetable stock, kept simmering

50 g/2 oz freshly grated Parmigiano Reggiano

sea salt and freshly milled black pepper

Serves 4

First prepare the artichokes by removing all the external leaves. Cut the artichokes in half and then into quarters. Rub the cut artichokes thoroughly with the lemon quarters to prevent oxidization. Remove the chokes and cut the artichokes into thin strips. Put the sliced artichokes into a basin of cold water with the lemon quarters until required.

Melt half the butter in a large pan and fry the onion gently with the prosciutto and the parsley until the onion is soft. Drain and dry the artichokes carefully, then add them to the onion. Stir and simmer gently, basting occasionally with the wine. Season with salt and pepper and, when the artichokes are soft, add the rice and stir until the rice is crackling hot.

Pour in 3 ladlefuls of stock and stir to allow the rice to absorb the liquid, then add the next ladleful. Continue stirring and adding stock until the rice is tender and creamy, but still firm to the bite.

Remove from the heat and stir in the remaining butter and the Parmigiano Reggiano. Adjust the seasoning, cover and rest for about 3 minutes. Transfer on to a warmed platter and serve at once.

Any edible flowers will work for this risotto, although the flavours will remain very subtle and delicate whatever you use. A combination of marigold petals, pansies, nasturtiums and violets will look very pretty.

Be careful when picking and choosing flowers that you use only those that are really edible.

Risotto with Edible Flowers

Risotto ai Fiori

1 small leek, trimmed and very finely chopped

40 g/1½ oz tablespoons unsalted butter

350 g/13 oz Arborio rice

1 glass dry white wine

up to 2 litres/8 cups delicate vegetable stock, kept simmering

50 g/2 oz freshly grated Parmigiano Reggiano

2 handfuls freshly picked edible flowers and their petals, washed and dried

sea salt and freshly milled black pepper

Serves 4

Melt half the butter in a large pan and fry the leek very gently until completely soft but not browned. Add the rice and stir constantly for about 5 minutes, until crackling hot but not browned.

Add the wine and continue to stir for a minute or so while the alcohol cooks off, then add about 3 ladlefuls of stock, stirring until the rice has absorbed almost all the liquid. Reduce the heat and continue to add the stock a ladleful at a time, stirring continuously and waiting until almost all the liquid has been absorbed before adding more stock.

When the rice is tender but firm to the bite, remove the pan from the heat and stir in the remaining butter and the Parmigiano Reggiano. Adjust the seasoning and leave to rest for about 4 minutes. Stir in one handful of the flowers and then arrange the risotto on a warmed serving dish, scattered with the remaining flowers. Serve at once.

This risotto looks really stunning if you finish off with a few courgette flowers or slices of courgette (zucchini) that have been deep-fried in batter and arranged on the top of the risotto just before it goes to the table. The crisp, golden batter looks and tastes fantastic against the smooth, sweet, creaminess of the risotto.

Risotto with Courgettes and their Flowers

Risotto con Zucchine e Fiori

7 tender young courgettes (zucchini), with their flowers, if possible

5 tablespoons extra virgin olive oil

300 g/11 oz risotto rice

up to 2 litres/8 cups vegetable or chicken stock, kept simmering

25 g/1 oz unsalted butter

60 g/2$^{1}/_{2}$ oz freshly grated Parmigiano Reggiano

sea salt and freshly milled pepper

Serves 6

Trim the courgettes and their flowers and slice very finely then heat the oil in a wide, deep pan and fry the sliced courgettes and their flowers until tender. Add the rice and stir to coat it with the oil. Cook it for about 5 minutes, stirring all the time, until the rice is hot and crackling.

Add some seasoning and then begin to add the hot stock a ladleful at a time, stirring constantly to prevent sticking and only adding more liquid when the rice has absorbed the previous quantity.

After about 20 minutes, and when the rice is tender but firm to the bite, remove the pan from the heat, adjust the seasoning and stir in the butter and cheese. Cover and rest for 2 minutes, then transfer onto a warmed platter to serve immediately.

A real classic. The bitterness of the radicchio is off-set by the sweetness imparted by the onion, butter, sugar and red wine. You can substitute Belgian Endive in this recipe.

Risotto with Radicchio

Risotto al Radicchio

1 large red onion, peeled and finely chopped

3 heads of radicchio, 2 heads finely shredded, 1 head washed and dried

50 g/2 oz unsalted butter

350 g/13 oz Arborio rice

1 glass dry red wine

up to 2 litres/8 cups chicken or vegetable stock, kept simmering

2 tablespoons vegetable oil

1 teaspoon granulated sugar

60 g/2½ oz freshly grated Parmigiano Reggiano

sea salt and freshly milled black pepper

Serves 4

Heat half the butter in a large pan and very gently fry the onion with the 2 shredded radicchio heads. When both the onion and the radicchio are soft, but not browned, add the rice and cook the grains until they are crackling hot.

After 3–4 minutes, add the red wine and stir until the alcohol has evaporated, then add 3 ladlefuls of hot stock. Stirring continuously, allow the rice to absorb almost all the liquid. Then, lower the heat and add another ladleful of stock, making sure the rice has absorbed all the liquid before adding any more.

Meanwhile, cut the washed whole head of radicchio into quarters, keeping the root end intact so that the leaves don't fall apart. Heat the vegetable oil in a shallow pan and quickly fry the radicchio on all sides until it is just soft. Sprinkle with the sugar and a little salt and pepper. Set aside and keep warm.

When the rice is tender but still firm to the bite, take the pan off the heat and stir in the remaining butter, 4 tablespoons of the Parmigiano Reggiano, and season to taste. Cover and leave to rest for about 4 minutes. Transfer to a warmed platter and arrange the braised radicchio on top, then sprinkle with the remaining cheese and serve at once.

This was the first thing I ever ate at Rhubarb, a restaurant in Johannesburg. For this dish to work well, it is important that the mushrooms are not too strong or overpowering, otherwise the flavour of the asparagus will be lost. For this reason, the mushrooms need to be fresh and not dried. In the absence of fresh wild mushrooms, use cultivated mushrooms with plenty of flavour, which are less overpowering than their wild cousins.

Risotto with Wild Mushroom and Asparagus
Risotto di Funghi con Asparagi

40 g/1½ oz unsalted butter

2 shallots, peeled and finely chopped

200 g/7 oz fresh wild mushrooms, cleaned and finely sliced

350 g/13 oz Arborio or Carnaroli rice

a small glass dry white wine

up to 2 litres/8 cups chicken or vegetable stock, kept simmering

a bunch of asparagus, tips only (use the stems for flavouring the stock if you wish)

50 g/2 oz freshly grated Parmigiano Reggiano

sea salt and freshly milled black pepper

Serves 4

Melt half the butter in a large pan and gently fry the shallots in half the butter with the mushrooms until both the shallots and the mushrooms are cooked, stirring frequently.

Add the rice and cook the grains thoroughly for about 3–4 minutes until they are very hot. Add the wine and stir for a further minute, then add 3 ladlefuls of hot stock and stir until most of the liquid has been absorbed by the rice. Then lower the heat and continue to cook, adding stock gradually and stirring the rice while it absorbs the liquid.

After about 15 minutes, add the asparagus tips and stir them through. As soon as the rice is tender but firm to the bite, take the risotto off the heat and stir in the remaining butter and three-quarters of the Parmigiano Reggiano. Taste and adjust the seasoning, then add a little bit more stock and cover. Leave to rest for 4 minutes, then stir once more before transferring on to a warm dish to serve, sprinkled lightly with the last of the cheese.

It's amazing how widely available salmon has become! Always try to look for fish that is wild or has been farmed with care and be prepared to spend a little bit more to get really good fish.

Risotto with Salmon
Risotto al Salmone

400 g /14 oz salmon tail fillet	Wash and check the fish, removing any visible bones. Put the bay leaf, salt, peppercorns, lemon peel and parsley into a saucepan large enough to take the fish and cover with water. Simmer the herbs gently for about 20 minutes then lower the salmon into the water. Poach for about 10 minutes, then cover the pan and take it off the heat. Leave the salmon to stand in the water until cooked.
1 bay leaf	
sea salt	
5 black peppercorns	
grated peel of ½ lemon	
a handful of parsley	Remove the fish from the pan then skin and fillet it carefully and then cut the flesh into small pieces. Strain and reserve the stock, then keep it simmering. Make sure you have up to 2 litres of stock. Add fish stock if necessary.
75 g/3 oz unsalted butter	
1 garlic clove, chopped	
1 tablespoon olive oil	Melt half the butter with the oil in a large pan and fry the garlic until just softened. Add the rice and toast the grains thoroughly, then add the wine. Cook the rice for 2–3 minutes until the alcohol has evaporated, then start to add the hot salmon stock, stirring constantly and always allowing the liquid to be absorbed before adding more.
400 g/14 oz Vialone Nano rice	
1 glass dry white wine	

To serve

2 tablespoons finely chopped fresh parsley

zest of a very small lemon

2 slices smoked salmon, cut into fine strips

Serves 4

Five minutes before the rice is cooked, stir in the cooked fish, breaking some up as you stir it through. When the rice is tender but still firm to the bite, take the pan off the heat and stir in the butter. Cover and leave to rest for 2 minutes, then transfer to a warmed platter. Sprinkle with the chopped parsley, lemon zest and the tiny strips of smoked salmon to serve.

This is quite a sophisticated ristotto that would be good for a special lunch or supper. It is important to use good fish stock, although it should not be so strong that it overpowers the delicate flavour of the asparagus.

Risotto with Prawns and Asparagus

Risotto con Gamberetti e Asparagi

40 g/1½ oz unsalted butter

2 small shallots, finely chopped

350 g/13 oz Carnaroli or Vialone Nano rice

1 glass dry white wine

2 litres/8 cups mild fish stock, kept simmering

20 asparagus spears, woody stems removed and steamed until just tender

200 g/7 oz cooked peeled prawns (shrimp)

sea salt and freshly milled salt and pepper

To garnish

a few whole, hot, steamed asparagus spears

a handful of cooked, warm prawns (shrimp)

Serves 4

Melt the butter in a large pan and gently fry the shallots until they are softened but not browned. Add the rice and stir with the other ingredients to toast the grains without browning them. After about 5 minutes, add the wine and stir for about 2 minutes. Then add 3 ladlefuls of hot stock and stir until the rice has absorbed all the liquid.

Continue to add the stock and stir it in, only adding more liquid when the previous amount has been absorbed. After about 15 minutes, about 5 minutes before the end of the cooking time, add the asparagus spears and prawns then continue to cook the risotto as before, taking care not to break up the asparagus spears or the prawns. Taste, then season with salt and pepper.

When the rice grains are tender but firm to the bite, and the texture is creamy, remove the pan from the heat and stir in the rest of the butter. Cover and leave to rest for 4 minutes, then stir again before transferring to a warmed dish. Serve at once, garnished with the extra asparagus spears and cooked, warm prawns.

This atypical risotto brings a delicious combination of flavours that
are much enjoyed at Rhubarb, a restaurant in Sandton,
Johannnesburg, and adapted here by me! Thank you Tod!

Risotto with Fresh Ginger and Mussels

Risotto con le Cozze e lo Zenzero Fresco

**1 x 10 cm (4 in)
piece of fresh (root)
ginger, peeled,
halved and very
finely chopped**

**5 garlic cloves, very
finely sliced**

**2 tablespoons extra
virgin olive oil**

**1 kg/2 lb 4 oz fresh
mussels, thoroughly
cleaned**

**2 glasses dry white
wine**

**a large handful fresh
flat leaf parsley,
coarsely chopped**

**40 g/1½ oz
unsalted butter**

**2 garlic cloves, finely
chopped**

**350 g/13 oz
Carnaroli rice**

**1 litre/4 cups fish
stock, kept simmering**

**2 tablespoons very
finely chopped fresh
coriander (cilantro)**

**sea salt and freshly
milled black pepper**

Serves 4

Fry the ginger very gently with the sliced garlic and the oil in a very
large saucepan until just softened. Add the mussels, the white wine and
the parsley and mix together thoroughly. Cover and steam for 8 minutes,
or until the mussels have all opened, then remove from the heat. When
the mussels are cool enough to handle, remove the meat from their
shells and reserve. Leave a few mussels on the shell to use as a garnish.
Discard any mussels that have not opened. Strain and reserve the
cooking liquid and keep hot.

Melt half the butter in a large pan and fry the chopped garlic until soft
but not browned, then add rice and stir until crackling hot. Add the
reserved liquid from the mussels and stir. When almost all the liquid
has been absorbed, begin adding the stock. Add a ladleful at a time
stirring continuously and only adding more when the rice has absorbed
each quantity of liquid.

Keep going in this way until the rice is tender but firm to the bite, then
stir in the reserved shelled mussels and season to taste. Remove the
pan from the heat, stir in the remaining butter and cover. Leave to rest
for 4 minutes, then stir again, adding a little more stock if required so
that the texture of the risotto is not too dry. Transfer onto a warmed
platter and sprinkle with the chopped coriander. Garnish with the
reserved mussels on their shells and serve at once.

Fish and Meat

If you have never cleaned scallops yourself before, be warned that it
is a fiddly and labour-intensive job! It's far better to buy scallops
which are clean and ready to use.

Risotto with Scallops

Risotto con le Capesante

**1.5 kg/3 lb 5 oz
scallops in their
shells, cleaned**

**100 g/4 oz
unsalted butter**

**3 shallots,
finely chopped**

4 tablespoons brandy

**300 g/11 oz
Carnaroli rice**

**up to 2 litres/8 cups
fish stock, kept
simmering**

**2 tablespoons finely
chopped fresh flat leaf
parsley**

**3 tablespoons double
(heavy) cream**

**sea salt and freshly
milled black pepper**

Serves 6

Clean the scallops and discard the shells, remove the roe from the white
flesh. If the scallops are very big, cut them in half.

Melt half the butter in a large pan and fry the shallots gently until soft.
Meanwhile, heat the remaining butter in a separate pan and quickly
fry the scallops for 2–3 minutes each side. Pour over the brandy and
set it alight. Season and remove the pan from the heat. Set aside
until required.

Add the rice to the soft shallots and mix together until the rice is
crackling hot and shiny. Pour in a ladleful of hot stock. Stir and allow
the grains to absorb the liquid, then add another ladleful and repeat.
Continue in this way for about fifteen minutes or until the rice is nearly
cooked. Add the cooked scallops and all their juices, the corals and the
parsley. Stir together and continue cooking the risotto as before.

When the risotto is creamy and velvety but the grains are still firm to
the bite, take the pan off the heat. Stir in the cream, cover and leave
the risotto to rest for about 2 minutes. Transfer to a warmed platter and
serve at once.

Although it isn't vital, having a pestle and mortar will help to make the lobster stock really flavoursome. Without a rich stock you will get a much blander flavour. To make crab risotto, follow this recipe but use three very large crabs instead of the two lobsters. This is a very long winded and labour-intensive recipe – you have been warned!

Risotto with Lobster

Risotto all'Aragosta

121

2 medium-sized lobsters, boiled and halved

100 g/4 oz unsalted butter

1 celery stick, coarsely chopped

1 carrot, coarsely chopped

1 onion, coarsely chopped

a handful of coarsely chopped fresh flat leaf parsley,

a sprig of fresh tarragon

4 tablespoons Marsala or brandy

2 shallots, very finely chopped

350 g/13 oz Carnaroli rice

1.2 litres/5 cups fish stock

a few drops of Tabasco sauce

sea salt and freshly milled black pepper

Serves 4

First, make the stock. Carefully remove all the white and dark meat, and any roe from the lobsters, then set aside. Make sure you discard all the inedible parts of the crustaceans.

Using a pestle and mortar or a very powerful food processor, pound the carcasses into a coarse puree. Put this mixture into a deep pan with half the butter, the celery, carrot, onion and herbs. Fry all this together until the vegetables are soft. Pour in the Marsala or brandy and set alight so the alcohol burns off. Pour in about a litre (4 cups) of water. Season with salt and pepper.

Heat the stock gently, then simmer, uncovered, for about 1 hour, stirring occasionally. Cool and strain carefully. There should be about 500 ml (2½ cups) of very intensely-flavoured stock. Put the lobster stock into a clean pan and heat until just simmering. In a separate pan, heat the fish stock until it is also just at simmering point.

In a third pan, melt the remaining butter and gently fry the shallots until soft. Add the rice and fry until the grains are shiny and crackling hot. Add a ladleful of the lobster stock and wait for it to be absorbed as you gently stir, then add a ladleful of the fish stock and stir in the same way until almost all the liquid is absorbed. Continue alternating ladlefuls of lobster and fish stock until the rice is about three-quarters cooked. Then add all the lobster meat and any roe then stir thoroughly to combine with the rice.

Continue adding the stocks and cooking the rice until the risotto is creamy, tender and velvety, but the grains are still firm to the bite. Take the pan off the heat and stir in the Tabasco sauce. Adjust the seasoning, stir and cover. Leave the risotto to rest for about 3 minutes, then turn onto a warmed platter and serve at once.

This black squid ink risotto is very dramatic in appearance but definitely not to everybody's taste! As well as buying whole cuttlefish with their own ink, you can buy squid ink in little sachets from good fishmongers and specialist food shops. Traditionally, the texture of this particular risotto is more soupy. If you are wondering what it tastes like, squid ink is intensely fishy and rather sweet.

Risotto with Squid Ink

Risotto con il Nero di Seppia

750 g/1 lb 8 oz cuttlefish with ink sacs

3 tablespoons extra virgin olive oil

½ onion, finely chopped

1 garlic clove, finely chopped

500 g/1 lb 2 oz Vialone Nano rice

125 ml/½ cup dry white wine

up to 2 litres/8 cups fish stock, kept simmering

12 g/½ oz unsalted butter

sea salt and freshly milled black pepper

3 tablespoons finely chopped fresh flat leaf parsley

Serves 4

Rinse the cuttlefish then remove the tentacles and head. Carefully remove the ink sacs from the heads taking care not split the sacs. Discard the yellow sac. Put the ink into a sieve or strainer over a small bowl and use the back of a teaspoon to press out the ink. Pour a few tablespoons of the fish stock over the sacs and leave to drain and so help to extract the rest of the ink.

Prepare the cuttlefish by removing all the internal organs and the back bone. Wash thoroughly and cut the flesh into thin rings and strips.

In a large pan, fry the onion and garlic in the olive oil until translucent and soft but not brown. Add the cuttlefish and cook gently for about 20 minutes, or until tender. Add all the rice and stir together thoroughly.

When the grains are hot and crackling, add the wine and the ink. Stir together and begin to add the stock, one ladleful at a time. Keep stirring, remembering to allow one portion of liquid to be absorbed before adding any more.

As soon as the risotto is cooked (about 20 minutes) and the rice is tender but firm to the bite, take the risotto off the heat and stir in the butter, salt, pepper, parsley and finish off with a final ladle of hot stock. Cover and leave to rest for 2–3 minutes, then stir again and turn out onto warmed plates or a platter to serve.

You can use either canned or cooked fresh crab for this recipe, and honestly the canned works very well indeed. Slightly sweet in flavour, and very uncharacteristic, this is a deliciously un-Italian tasting risotto.

Risotto with Crab and Coconut Cream

Risotto alla Crema di Cocco con il Granchio

40 g/1 ½ oz unsalted butter

1 onion, finely chopped

½ teaspoon mild curry powder

½ tablespoon finely chopped tender lemon grass

350 g/13 oz Arborio rice

2 litres/8 cups light fish stock, kept simmering

250 g/9 oz cooked crab meat, flaked

150 ml/²⁄₃ cup coconut cream

2 tablespoons chopped fresh coriander (cilantro) leaves

sea salt and freshly milled black pepper

Serves 4

Melt half the butter in a large pan and fry the onion very gently with the curry powder and lemongrass. When the onion is soft but not browned, add the rice and stir for about 5 minutes.

When the rice is crackling hot, add 3 ladlefuls of hot stock and stir until the rice has absorbed most of the liquid. Lower the heat and continue adding the stock and stirring until each ladleful has been absorbed by the rice before adding the next.

When the rice is tender but still firm to the bite, mix in the crab meat, the remaining butter and the coconut cream. Season to taste and stir before leaving to rest, covered, for about 4 minutes. Stir again and serve in warmed bowls or on a warmed serving dish, sprinkled with the coriander.

You can follow this recipe using lobster, prawns, langoustines or white fish as possible variants. If coconut cream is unavailable, use dairy cream and substitute parsley for the coriander.

I'll give you a basic outline of the right quantities to use for this symphony of flavours, but you must not feel at all restricted. Feel free to use whatever seafood you think is appropriate and looks delicious at the time.

Risotto With Seafood

Risotto Con i Frutti di Mare

500 g/l lb 2 oz vongole (baby clams) washed and scrubbed clean

500 g/l lb 2 oz mussels, washed and scrubbed clean

250 g/8 oz white fish fillet

250 g/8 oz raw, shell-on small prawns (shrimp)

250 g/8 oz raw, shell-on langoustines or large prawns (shrimp)

1 crab, cooked and split open

1 bottle dry white wine

150 ml/²/₃ cup extra virgin olive oil

¹/₂ dried red chilli pepper, finely chopped

3 garlic cloves, finely chopped

3 tablespoons chopped fresh parsley

500 g/1 lb 2 oz Carnaroli rice

1.2 litres/5 cups strong fish stock, kept simmering

sea salt and freshly milled black pepper

Serves 4 to 6

First, cook the seafood. Wash and clean all the shellfish really carefully. Place the vongole in a deep pan with a glass of dry white wine, cover and steam open the shellfish. Remove three-quarters of the vongole from their shells. Set them aside along with the vongole still in their shells. Strain the juices from the pan through a fine sieve and into a bowl. Next, do exactly the same with the mussels, also straining and reserving the cooking liquor.

Then, put 2 tablespoons of the oil into a shallow pan and fry the fish fillet on both sides, basting with the wine to keep it very soft. Season with salt and pepper and flake it roughly. Set aside until required. Heat 3 tablespoons of olive oil in another pan and quickly fry the prawns until bright pink and cooked through, turning frequently and basting with wine. Peel the prawns and add the shells and heads to the simmering fish stock.

Heat a further 3 tablespoons of olive oil and quickly fry the langoustines until cooked through, turning frequently and basting with wine. When they are cooked through, take them out of the pan. Remove the legs and claws then open them out, removing all the flesh.

Put the reserved flesh with the peeled prawns for later use. Discard any inedible parts, such as the intestinal tube and the empty claws, legs and carcasses to the stock. (If you are using giant prawns, simply peel half and leave the other half with the shell on, adding the removed shells to the fish stock.)

Remove all the dark and white meat from the crab's body, taking care to leave all the inedible parts in the shell. Reserve the claws. Do not add the crab shell to the stock.

Heat the remaining oil in a large pan and fry the chilli, garlic and parsley together for 2 minutes, then add the rice. Stir thoroughly with the other ingredients until the rice is crackling hot, then add a glass of wine.

Stir for 2 minutes while the alcohol evaporates, then add the cooking juices from the clams and mussels. Stir and allow the grains to absorb the liquid, then begin to add alternately the wine and hot stock, which will need to be strained, into the risotto. When the wine has been used, continue with only stock.

Continue in this way until the risotto is nearly cooked, then add all the cooked seafood and fish including the shells, legs and claws. Stir together thoroughly and continue to cook as before gradually adding the final quantities of fish stock and stirring while the rice absorbs the liquid. When the rice is creamy but still firm to the bite, transfer the risotto onto a warmed platter and arrange it so that all the claws and shells are on the top. Serve at once.

A delicate, summery risotto that is ideal for a summer dinner party.
Its elegance and subtle flavour make it particularly special.

Risotto with Salmon Roe and Watercress

Risotto con le Uova di Salmone e il Crescione

1 mild onion, finely chopped

40 g/1½ oz unsalted butter

350 g/13 oz Vialone Nano rice

1 glass dry white wine

up to 2 litres/8 cups light vegetable stock, kept simmering

25 g/1 oz freshly grated Parmigiano Reggiano

3 handfuls of watercress leaves, washed dried and coarsely chopped

4 tablespoons salmon roe

a few sprigs of watercress, to garnish

sea salt and freshly milled black pepper

Serves 4

Melt half the butter in a large pan and fry the onion gently until very soft but not coloured. Add all the rice and cook the grains for about 5 minutes until crackling hot. Add the wine and stir for 1 minute, then add 3 ladlefuls of stock and stir until the rice has absorbed the liquid. Lower the heat and continue to add the stock 1½ ladlefuls at a time, making sure that the rice has absorbed the liquid before adding any more stock.

When the rice is tender but still firm to the bite, remove the pan from the heat and stir in the Parmigiano Reggiano and the remaining butter. Then add the watercress and stir through. Taste and adjust the seasoning, adding a final ladle of hot stock. Cover and rest for about 4 minutes, then stir again. Very gently stir through the salmon roe before serving with a sprig of watercress to garnish.

If watercress is hard to find, use tender young salad leaves instead, or lettuce hearts shredded coarsely.

Bottarga is the cured roe of large fish that has been dried and salted so it can be shaved or grated. Most common varieties of bottarga come from mullet, tuna, swordfish or bass. It is traditionally a Sardinian speciality, although it is also found in other parts of southern Italy. The strong, almost overpowering taste means it must be used sparingly. You can buy it either in jars, ready-grated, or whole as a block. It is expensive ingredient, though the price varies according to which fish it comes from.

Risotto with Bottarga

Risotto con la Bottarga

1 onion, very finely chopped

3 tablespoons extra virgin olive oil

350 g/13 oz Arborio or Vialone Nano rice

1 large glass dry white wine

up to 2 litres/8 cups fish stock, kept simmering

a handful of chopped, fresh flat leaf parsley

1 teaspoon fresh lemon juice

1 teaspoon freshly grated lemon zest

75 g/3 oz Bottarga

sea salt and freshly milled black pepper

extra virgin olive oil, to drizzle

Serves 4

Fry the onion very gently in the olive oil until soft but not browned at all. Add the rice and toast thoroughly in the hot oil until it is crackling hot.

Add the white wine and stir for a minute or so to allow the alcohol to evaporate. Then add 3 ladlefuls of stock and stir until the rice has absorbed most of the liquid, then add more stock and continue to cook. Add about $1\frac{1}{2}$ ladlefuls of stock at a time and always wait for the stock to be absorbed before adding more.

After about 20 minutes, the rice should be tender but firm to the bite. Take the pot off the heat and stir in the parsley and adjust the seasoning. Add the lemon juice and zest, another ladleful of stock and cover. Leave to rest for 4 minutes, then stir again and transfer onto a warmed serving dish. Sprinkle with the grated or shaved Bottarga and drizzle lightly with the olive oil to serve.

Bresaola is air-dried, salted beef that is sold in wafer-thin slices and usually served as an antipasti, drizzled with olive oil and lemon juice. In this risotto, the bresaola is sliced and fried, intensifying the flavour and adding depth to the wine-enriched risotto. Take care not to add too much extra salt as the meat is quite salty too.

Risotto with Bresaola
Risotto alla Bresaola

40 g/1½ oz unsalted butter

1 small onion, very finely chopped

250 g/9 oz thinly sliced bresaola

350 g/13 oz Arborio or Carnaroli rice

2 large glasses dry red wine

up to 2 litres/8 cups chicken or vegetable stock, kept simmering

40 g/1½ oz freshly grated Parmigiano Reggiano

sea salt and freshly milled black pepper

Serves 6

Melt half the butter in a large pan and fry the onion gently. When the onion is soft, cut the bresaola into strips and add half to the pan and fry for a few minutes. Add all the rice and mix with the other ingredients in the pan until it is crackling hot.

After about 4 minutes, when the rice is well toasted and shiny, add the wine and stir quickly for 2 minutes to evaporate the alcohol and allow the rice to absorb the wine. Next, add 1 or 2 ladlefuls of the simmering stock and continue to stir constantly, only adding more stock when the previous liquid has been absorbed.

The risotto will be ready after about 20 minutes, when the rice is tender but still firm to the bite. Take the pan off the heat and stir in the remaining Bresaola and butter and half the cheese. Stir vigorously and adjust the seasoning as necessary. Cover and rest for 3 minutes, then transfer onto a warm platter and sprinkle with the rest of the cheese. Serve at once.

I prefer to use wild duck for this dish as it tends to be less fatty. I would also strongly recommend that you ask the butcher or game dealer to bone the duck for you and get him to give you the carcass and skin for your stock. Alternatively, use 4 to 5 skinned small duck breasts.

Risotto with Duck

Risotto all'Anatra

1 duck weighing about 2 kg/2 lb 4 oz, preferably boned

5 tablespoons extra virgin olive oil

2 garlic cloves, lightly crushed

2 onions, finely chopped

4 fresh sage leaves

1/2 bottle dry white wine

1 tablespoon tomato purée

75 g/3 oz unsalted butter

300 g/11 oz Carnaroli rice

up to 2 litres/8 cups rich duck stock, kept simmering

40 g/1 1/2 oz freshly grated Parmigiano Reggiano

sea salt and freshly milled black pepper

Serves 4

Trim all the duck meat and cut it into evenly sized cubes. Heat the oil in a large pan and fry the garlic and onions until soft and translucent. Add the sage and the duck and brown the meat all over. Raise the heat, then add the wine and mix thoroughly, allowing the alcohol to burn off before mixing in the tomato purée, half the butter and the seasoning. Cover and simmer until the duck is tender, occasionally adding a little more wine or water to prevent sticking.

When the duck is cooked, add all the rice to the pan and stir thoroughly. Begin to add the hot stock a ladleful at a time, stirring constantly and allowing the liquid to be absorbed by the rice before adding more.

When the risotto is creamy and the rice is tender but still firm to the bite, remove it from the heat and stir in the remaining butter and the Parmigiano Reggiano. Adjust the seasoning and cover. Leave to rest for 2 minutes, then transfer on to a warmed platter and serve at once.

The rich flavour of the ham combines extremely well with the rice, the white wine and the stock to make a fantastically creamy risotto that you will want to make again and again. As Parma ham is quite salty you might not need to add extra salt

Risotto with Parma Ham

Risotto al Prosciutto di Parma

1 small onion, very finely chopped

50 g/2 oz unsalted butter, plus 1 tablespoon

250 g/9 oz thinly sliced Parma ham

300 g/11 oz Arborio or Carnaroli rice

1 large glass dry white wine

up to 2 litres/8 cups chicken or pork and vegetable stock, kept simmering

75 g/3 oz freshly grated Parmigiano Reggiano

salt and freshly milled black pepper

Serves 4

Melt the 2 oz of butter in a large pan and fry the onion gently until soft, taking care not to let it colour. Chop the Parma ham into strips and, when the onion is soft, add half to the pan and fry for a few minutes; then add the rice.

Cook the rice, turning it frequently in the butter until very hot. After about 4 minutes, when the rice is well toasted and shiny, add the wine and stir quickly for 2 minutes to evaporate the alcohol, then add 1 or 2 ladlefuls of hot stock. Continue to stir constantly, only adding more stock when the previous liquid has been absorbed. The risotto will be ready after 20 minutes.

When the rice is tender but still firm to the bite, take the risotto off the heat and stir in the remaining ham, the tablespoon of butter and half the Parmigiano Reggiano. Stir vigorously and adjust seasoning as necessary. Cover and rest for 3 minutes, then transfer onto a warm platter and sprinkle with the rest of the cheese. Serve at once.

The traditional recipe for this much loved risotto includes beef bone marrow, which in recent times has been an extremely contentious ingredient. If you are concerned, use organic beef bone marrow for this recipe. A marrow-free version of the recipe can be found on p 20.

Classic Milanese Saffron Risotto

Risotto alla Milanese Classico

½ onion, finely chopped

75 g/3 oz unsalted butter

40 g/1½ oz raw beef bone marrow, chopped

300 g/11 oz Vialone Gigante or other risotto rice

up to 2 litres/8 cups rich stock (traditionally made with veal, beef and chicken, assorted vegetables but no tomato), kept simmering

1 sachet of saffron powder

50 g/2 oz freshly grated Parmigiano Reggiano

Serves 4

Soak the onion in cold water for about 10 minutes, then drain and squeeze dry in a napkin. Melt the butter in a large pan and fry the onion very slowly with the beef marrow. When the onion is soft, add the rice. Stir to coat the grains in the butter and onions and cook until the rice is crackling hot but not coloured.

Begin to add the hot stock a ladleful at a time stirring constantly and allowing the liquid to be absorbed before adding more. Continue to cook the rice in this way, making sure that the rice always absorbs the stock before you add more liquid.

About half way through the cooking time (approximately 10 minutes) add the saffron powder and mix thoroughly in to the rice. When the risotto is creamy and velvety, but the rice grains are still firm to the bite, take the pan off the heat.

Stir in the rest of the butter and the cheese. Cover and rest for a 2–3 minutes, then stir again and transfer onto a warmed platter. Serve at once, offering extra grated Parmigiano Reggiano at the table.

Both the red wine and the nutty taste of the rice wonderfully compliment the gamey flavour of the pigeon. This is a risotto that takes slightly longer to cook than usual, as the pigeon breast can be tough and will need more time than the rice.

Risotto with Pigeon Breast and Red Wine

Risotto al Piccione con il Vino Rosso

6 plump pigeon (squab) breasts, trimmed and skinned

1 bottle dry, full-bodied red wine

2 bay leaves

1 clove

1 onion, sliced

peel of ¹/₂ orange

3 tablespoons extra virgin olive oil

2 shallots, very finely chopped

40 g/1¹/₂ oz unsalted butter

350 g/13 oz Carnaroli rice

up to 2 litres/8 cups game or chicken stock, kept simmering

¹/₂ teaspoon finely grated orange zest

¹/₂ teaspoon fresh rosemary leaves, very finely chopped

40 g/1¹/₂ oz freshly grated Parmigiano Reggiano

sea salt and freshly milled black pepper

Serves 4

Lay the pigeon breasts in a non-metallic container and pour over the red wine so the meat is covered. Add the bay leaves, clove, sliced onion and orange peel. Leave to marinate for about 4 hours, then strain, reserving all the liquid.

Heat the oil in a pan and fry the pigeon breasts to seal them for about 3 minutes on each side. Remove the pigeon from the pan and slice very thinly into long strips. Return to the pan and lower the heat then pour over enough of the reserved wine to cover the meat. Simmer very gently for about 45 minutes or until the pigeon is completely tender, adding more wine, if required.

Melt half the butter in a large pan and gently fry the shallots until softened but not browned. Add the rice and toast the grains until very hot, stirring frequently, for about 5 minutes. Pour in half the remaining reserved marinating wine and stir for about 2 minutes, then add the pigeon.

Add about 1¹/₂ ladlefuls of stock at a time and continue to cook, stirring, and waiting for the rice to absorb the liquid before adding more. As soon as the is tender but still firm to the bit, remove the pan from the heat, stir in the remaining butter, the rosemary and the grated orange zest. Mix in the Parmigiano Reggiano and adjust the seasoning, then cover and leave to rest for about 4 minutes. Stir again and serve at once on warmed plates.

Fruit and Alcohol

I love pears poached in red wine until they are completely soft and dark, so I decided to create a risotto using this very special combination of tastes. The result is slightly unusual, but it is interesting and a worthy part of this collection.

Risotto with Pears and Red Wine

Risotto alle Pere con il Vino Rosso

50 g/2 oz unsalted butter

1 onion, peeled and chopped very finely

1 clove

300 g/11 oz risotto rice

2 glasses dry red wine

3 ripe pears, peeled, cored and cubed

up to 2 litres/8 cups vegetable stock, kept simmering

a large pinch of powdered cinnamon

sea salt and freshly milled black pepper

Serves 4

Melt half the butter in a large pan and gently fry the onion with the clove. When the onion is soft and melting, remove and discard the clove, add the rice and stir to thoroughly heat the grains.

When the rice is crackling hot, add the wine and cook, stirring, until the alcohol has evaporated and all the liquid has been absorbed. Add the pear and stir to combine with the rice.

As soon as the rice and pears are well blended and the grains have absorbed all the wine, add the first ladleful of hot stock. Stir until the stock has been absorbed and then add more stock. Continue in this way until the risotto is creamy and tender but still firm to the bite.

Remove the pan from the heat and stir in the cinnamon and the remaining butter. Season to taste, stir and then cover. Leave to rest for about 2 minutes, then stir again before transferring onto a warmed platter or individual plates to serve.

A good, late-night party risotto: a bit mad and wild yet still delicious and very soothing.

Risotto with Vodka and Orange

Risotto alla Vodka con Arancio

1 onion, finely chopped

50 g/2 oz unsalted butter

300 g/11 oz risotto rice

1 glass dry white wine

up to 2 litres/8 cups vegetable stock, kept simmering

juice and zest of 2 oranges

1/3 tumbler vodka

3 tablespoons single (light) cream

25 g/1 oz freshly grated Parmigiano Reggiano

sea salt and freshly milled black pepper

grated orange zest, to serve

Serves 4

Melt the butter in a large pan and fry the onion until it is soft. Add the rice and cook the grains until they are crackling hot, then add the wine and boil rapidly until the alcohol has evaporated.

When the wine has been absorbed into the rice, add the first ladleful of stock stirring constantly and allowing the liquid to be absorbed before adding more. Continue to cook the rice in this way, until all the stock has been added.

About 5 minutes before the risotto is cooked, stir in the orange juice and zest, and the vodka. When the risotto is creamy and tender, but still firm to the bite, take the pan off the heat and stir in the cream and Parmigiano Reggiano cheese. Stir through, cover and leave to rest for 2 minutes. To serve, transfer to a warmed serving dish and sprinkle with the grated orange zest.

A most unusual risotto flavoured with a little Gorgonzola and with just that final hit of Acquavite to make it really special. If you prefer, you can use pears instead of apples.

Risotto with Apple

Risotto con le Mele

75 g/3 oz unsalted butter

1 small onion, very finely chopped

300 g/11 oz risotto rice

1 glass dry white wine

500 g/1 lb 2 oz tart eating apples, cored and chopped

up to 2 litres/8 cups vegetable or chicken stock, kept simmering

75 g/3 oz Gorgonzola, diced

4 tablespoons Acquavite (optional)

sea salt and freshly milled black pepper

Serves 6

Melt the butter in a large pan and fry the onion gently until soft. Add the rice and cook the grains until shiny, opaque and crackling hot.

Add the wine and stir until the liquid has been absorbed and the alcohol has evaporated. Add the apple and mix with the rice, then add a little stock and stir until the liquid has been absorbed.

Continue to cook the risotto by adding a ladleful of hot stock at a time, only adding more when all the liquid has been absorbed. Stir the risotto constantly so that the liquid is evenly distributed and to prevent sticking.

About half way through the cooking time (when about half the stock has been used), add the Gorgonzola and stir until it has melted. Check the seasoning, bearing in mind the saltiness of the cheese, and continue to add the stock as before.

When the risotto is creamy and tender, but still firm to the bite, stir in the Acquavite and take the pan off the heat.

Stir in the remaining butter, cover the pan and leave the risotto to rest for about 2 minutes. Stir again and serve on a warmed platter or individual plates.

I first tasted this risotto in Sorrento, where the lemons grow big and fat in the shadow of Mount Vesuvius. I have since made it myself with lemons from other parts of the world, but like so many things in life, the first time will always be the best – and the most unforgettable. Please make sure you use unwaxed lemons!

Risotto with Lemon

Risotto al Limone

2 shallots or 1 leek (white only), very finely chopped

100 g/4 oz unsalted butter

350 g/13 oz risotto rice

1 large glass dry white wine

100 g/4 oz cubed full-fat cheese such as Bel Paese or Fontina

up to 2 litres/8 cups vegetable stock or light chicken stock, kept simmering

zest and juice of 2 small or 1 large lemon (unwaxed)

1 tablespoon Limoncello liqueur, optional

sea salt and freshly milled black pepper

freshly grated Parmigiano Reggiano, to serve

Serves 4

Melt half the butter in a large pan and fry the shallots very gently until soft and translucent. Add the rice and fry, making sure that the rice and shallots do not brown.

Add half the wine and stir until the liquid has been absorbed and the alcohol has evaporated. Add the rest of the wine and repeat as before.

Add the first ladleful of stock and the cubed cheese. Mix thoroughly and, when all the liquid has been absorbed, add another ladleful of stock, stirring constantly and allowing the liquid to be absorbed before adding more.

When the risotto is creamy and tender but firm to the bite, stir in the lemon zest, lemon juice and Limoncello. Allow the alcohol to boil off for 1 minute, then stir in the remaining butter. Check the seasoning, cover the pan and leave to rest for 1 minute, then transfer onto a warm dish and serve at once. Offer cheese separately.

This is a weird concept, I know, but actually it looks lovely and tastes even better – much more so than you might think!

Risotto with Strawberries

Risotto di Fragole

50 g/2 oz unsalted butter

1 small onion or 2 shallots, finely chopped

350 g/13 oz risotto rice

400 g/14 oz strawberries, washed and hulled

1½ large glasses red wine

up to 2 litres/8 cups chicken stock, kept simmering

4 tablespoons double (heavy) cream

50 g/2 oz freshly grated Parmigiano Reggiano

sea salt and plenty of freshly milled black pepper

a few strawberries, to decorate

Serves 4

Melt the butter in a large pan and fry the onion or shallots until soft and translucent. Add the rice and stir thoroughly to mix with the butter and onion.

Thinly slice half the strawberries and stir them into the rice, then add 1 glass of wine. Cook until the strawberries are pulpy, and some of the wine has evaporated.

Then add the second glass of wine and stir until the rice has absorbed the liquid. Next, start to add the hot stock a ladleful at a time, stirring continuously until the rice has absorbed all the liquid before adding any more.

About 3 minutes before the rice is done, stir in the remaining strawberries and cook until they break down slightly and become soft and pulpy. Stir in the cream, the Parmigiano Reggiano, a little salt and plenty of freshly milled black pepper. Allow the risotto to finish cooking, then arrange on a platter, decorate with a few strawberries and serve at once. Offer extra grated Parmigiano Reggiano at the table.

Index